Applying the Constructivist Approach to Cognitive Therapy

Applying the Constructivist Approach to Cognitive Therapy goes beyond the traditional objectivist approach of uncovering the *what* of a client's dysfunctional thinking by helping client and therapist understand *why* the client thinks in a dysfunctional manner. This unique work demonstrates how this thinking can be uncovered through dream work, analytic hypnotherapy, ecstatic trance, and other spontaneous trance experiences such as the use of imagination, free association, and guided imagery. Utilizing hypnotherapeutic techniques, the author shows how clients can reframe these thoughts to achieve a healthier, more functional way of thinking. Replete with case studies and practical guidance, this text will help therapists take clients beyond a simple resolution of their problems and offer an avenue to greater personal growth, maturity, and creativity.

Nicholas E. Brink, PhD, is a licensed clinical psychologist who operated a private practice for 22 years, offering services in marital psychotherapy and hypnosis. He is the past president of the American Association for the Study of Mental Imagery and past board member of the International Association for the Study of Dreams. Dr. Brink is semiretired and conducts research on the parallels between shamanic journeying, hypnosis, and dream work.

Nicholas Brink's book, *Applying the Constructivist Approach to Cognitive Therapy: Resolving the Unconscious Past*, is so relevant in the twenty-first century because people create their own realities due to social media technology, internet prevalence, and the ability to be exposed to thousands of information sites at the touch of a finger. The discussion of quantum physics is one of the most well-written explanations of its connections to psychology.

James M. Honeycutt, PhD, senior managing co-editor of
Imagination, Cognition, and Personality

Applying the Constructivist Approach to Cognitive Therapy
Resolving the Unconscious Past

Nicholas E. Brink

NEW YORK AND LONDON

First published 2019
by Routledge
52 Vanderbilt Avenue, New York, NY 10017

and by Routledge
2 Park Square, Milton Park, Abingdon, Oxon, OX14 4RN

Routledge is an imprint of the Taylor & Francis Group, an informa business

© 2019 Taylor & Francis

The right of Nicholas E. Brink to be identified as author of this work has been asserted by him in accordance with Sections 77 and 78 of the Copyright, Designs and Patents Act 1988.

All rights reserved. No part of this book may be reprinted or reproduced or utilised in any form or by any electronic, mechanical, or other means, now known or hereafter invented, including photocopying and recording, or in any information storage or retrieval system, without permission in writing from the publishers.

Trademark notice: Product or corporate names may be trademarks or registered trademarks, and are used only for identification and explanation without intent to infringe.

Library of Congress Cataloging-in-Publication Data
Names: Brink, Nicholas E., 1939- author.
Title: Applying the constructivist approach to cognitive therapy : resolving the unconscious past / Nicholas E. Brink.
Description: New York, NY : Routledge, 2019. | Includes bibliographical references and index. | Description based on print version record and CIP data provided by publisher; resource not viewed.
Identifiers: LCCN 2019006986 (print) | LCCN 2019007331 (ebook) | ISBN 9780429397714 (E-book) | ISBN 9780367028053 (hardback) | ISBN 9780367028060 (pbk.) | ISBN 9780429397714 (ebk)
Subjects: | MESH: Hypnosis–methods | Cognitive Behavioral Therapy–methods | Imagery (Psychotherapy) | Dreams–psychology
Classification: LCC RC489.C63 (ebook) | LCC RC489.C63 (print) | NLM WM 415 | DDC 616.89/1425–dc23
LC record available at https://lccn.loc.gov/2019006986

ISBN: 978-0-367-02805-3 (hbk)
ISBN: 978-0-367-02806-0 (pbk)
ISBN: 978-0-429-39771-4 (ebk)

Typeset in Garamond
by Swales & Willis, Exeter, Devon, UK

Contents

List of Illustrations   viii
Foreword   ix
Acknowledgements   xiii

1 **Constructivist vs. Objectivist Cognitive Therapy**   1

   The Automatic Thought 2
   Constructivist vs. Objectivist 4
   The Journey to Why 4
   Learning the More Functional Thoughts 6
   The Constructivist Alternative 7
   The Accuracy of the Words Used 8
   The Metaphoric Language of the Unconscious Mind 9
   Cognitive Therapy from a Psychoanalytic Perspective 11
   The Universal Mind Beyond 11

2 **Nighttime Dreams**   14

   The Nature of Dreams 14
   Dream Interpretation 16
   Remembering and Recording Dreams 18
   Dream Incubation 18
   The Course of Dream Work in Therapy 21
   Cognitive-Narrative Dream Work 22
   The Objectivist Approach to Dream Work 25
   Dreams Can Reflect Therapeutic Progress 26
   Lucid Dreaming 27

3 **Spontaneous Trance**   30

   Telling Your Story 30
   Focusing 31

Free Association 32
Imagination 34
Waking Morning Reverie 35
Self-Hypnosis 36
Guided Imagery 38

4 **Hypnosis as an Avenue into the Unconscious**   41

The Nature of Hypnosis 41
The Formal Induction of Hypnotic Trance 42
Dreaming and Hypnosis 44
Free Association, Imagination, and Hypnosis 45
Cognitive Therapy and Hypnosis 46
Hypnotic Susceptibility 46
Disorder Specific Hypnotherapy 47
Major Depression 48
Managing Anger 50
Another Hypnotherapeutic Approach to
   Cognitive-Behavioral Therapy 51
     Stress Inoculation Training (SIT) 52
     Exposure and Response Prevention (ERP) 52
     Problem Solving Therapy (PST) 52
     Cognitive Therapy 53

5 **Analytic Hypnotherapy**   56

The Affect Bridge and Age Regression 56
Beyond Catharsis 57
Molly 57
Dream Work and Analytic Hypnotherapy 62
Matt 66

6 **Ecstatic Trance**   69

Research of Felicitas Goodman 69
Induction of Ecstatic Trance 70
The Body Postures 71
Healing 72
Beyond the Unconscious 74
Spirits of the Earth 79

	Contents	vii
7	Ecstatic Soul Retrieval and Analytic Hypnotherapy	84

Ecstatic Soul Retrieval 84
Patricia 89
Integrating ESR and Analytic Hypnotherapy 96
Parallels between Analytic Hypnotherapy and the
   Ecstatic Postures 96
Chuck 98

8	Evidence for the Universal Mind	104

Rupert Sheldrake 104
Ervin Laszlo 107
Quantum Physics 110
The Power of Extrasensory Perception 110
   Dream Psi 111
   The Ganzfield Experiment 111
   Psychokinesis 112
   Unconscious Psychic Responses 112
   Two Additional Studies 113
Braden's Divine Matrix 115
   DNA Phantom Effect 115
   The Effect of Emotions on Isolated DNA 115
   The Effect of Coherent Emotions on Isolated DNA 116
   The Double Slit Experiment of Quantum Physics 116
   Non-Local Coherence 117

9	Evolution of Consciousness	119

Time-Free Transparency 120
Developmental Stages of Human Consciousness 121
The New Age 123

Index		128

Illustrations

2.1	Mayan Oracle	20
6.1	Nupe Diviner	73
6.2	Hallstatt Warrior	77
6.3	Bahia Metamorphosis	80
6.4	Jama-Coaque Diviner	82
7.1	Bear Spirit	85
7.2	Lady of Cholula Diviner	86
7.3	Olmec Diviner	88
7.4	Jivaro Under World	89
7.5	Feathered Serpent	90
7.6	Olmec Prince	91
7.7	Venus of Galgenberg	92

Foreword

As the senior, managing co-editor of the journal *Imagination, Cognition, and Personality*, I have known Nick Brink as a dedicated book review editor for the journal. I first met him at the annual conference of the American Association for the Study of Mental Imagery almost three decades ago. He is a consummate psychotherapist, reader, and a voracious writer, in his own right having authored numerous books dealing with ecstatic trance and therapy.

Nick Brink explores the evolutionary development of constructivist cognitive therapy with the critical examination of resolving people's past. The historical legacy of Aaron Beck and his pioneering work on automatic thought in psychotherapy and the acclaimed Beck Depression Inventory (1972; also see 2008) is discussed. Indeed, a word search finds 214 occurrences of the keyword of depression.

The constructivist approach to cognitive therapy is particularly relevant during the 21st century because individuals create their own realities due to social media technology, internet prevalence, and the ability to be exposed to thousands of information sites at the touch of a finger. George Herbert Kelly (1955) created the theory of personal constructs, better known as "constructivism" which presumes that individuals' sense of reality are constructed from life experience, rather than discovered by therapists.

The influences of constructivism are seen in humanistic, person-centered, cognitive behavioral, dialectical, and existential approaches to therapy. Constructivism utilizes a person-as-scientist approach in which people use personal constructs in the form of implicit hypotheses and theories to predict the behavior of others. Since people are implicit "lay" scientists, their constructs are continually tested and altered when individuals attempt new behaviors and consider new perspectives, whether this occurs in a therapy session or in daily life.

Nicholas Brink explores the evolutionary development of constructivist cognitive therapy with the critical examination of resolving people's past. The historical legacy of Aaron Beck and his pioneering work on automatic thought in psychotherapy and the mindfulness of cognitive therapy is provocatively discussed in this book. Beck (1983) proposed that the dialectical needs for sociotropy and autonomy are related to depression. Hence, excessive involvement in interpersonal relationships must be balanced with independence. This is similar to the secure attachment which balances the avoidant attachment style with the anxious/ambivalent style (Bekker and Croon, 2010; Allen et al., 2002).

Chapter 1 discusses Beck's premonitions on automatic thought and drawing on the work of Jean Piaget, Brink frames Beck's therapy as "objectivist cognitive therapy" as distinguished from Piaget's notion of constructivist where the mind is active rather than passive. Brink articulates how Beck is not concerned with *why* a patient thinks a certain way, but *what* is the patient's faulty way of thinking? I would argue (pun intended) that after tragedies, stressful episodes, the fundamental asking of the why question which is concerned with basic etiology, often provides the answers to the fundamental questions of who, what, where, when, and how. Collectively, these basic questions are referred to as the "five Ws and H" and are used to inquire about crises (see https://en.wikipedia.org/wiki/Five_Ws).

The mind has learned an association between the various symptoms. This means that when negative mood happens again (for any reason) it will tend to trigger all the other symptoms. When this happens, the old habits of negative thinking will start up again, negative thinking gets into the same rut, and a full-blown episode of depression may be the result.

The second chapter on dreams is intriguing; especially when Brink adds the admonition that most people dream for more than two hours a night and that recall can be enhanced "if they go to bed at night with the intent of recording their dreams upon waking." The case study of "Amy" dealing with PTSD in relation to having nightmares of her father beating her mother is interesting in terms of imagery rehearsal. Relatedly, rehearsal is a major function of daydreaming in the form of imagined interactions as individuals use visual and verbal imagery to envision solutions (Honeycutt, 2003, 2015). The discussion of how dream recall can reveal progress in therapy is enticing.

Everyday trance as we become lost in storytelling is discussed in the third chapter. Again, a case study is used in the case of "Matt" and he discusses his depression. It is intriguing how free association is enhanced through telling narratives when the storyteller realizes that there is active listening by another. Hence, listening intently can be cause and effect of insightful narratives in a reciprocal, closed loop. This reminds me of the classic work of Carl Rogers (1965) who is mentioned in the fourth chapter dealing with hypnotic trance. The origin of hypnosis as a learned skill is traced back to Bernheim's (1891) early definition of hypnosis in the 19th century in terms of "heighted suggestibility." Hence, suggestibility, listening, and problem solving can be instantiated through hypnotic trance. Relatedly, a type of cognitive reframing is common among biofeedback therapists who use nexus or heart math technology to monitor heart rate and physiological reactions for the treatment of stress disorders based on cybernetics (see https://stens-biofeedback.com/pages/what-is-biofeedback).

Chapter 5 covers analytic hypnotherapy. The affect bridge technique is summarized in terms of the linkage between emotions associated with a problem and carrying the associated emotion back in time using hypnotic age regression to identify the cause of the problem, as illustrated in the recurring case studies of Molly and Matt.

Chapter 6 outlines ecstatic trance. Nicholas has numerous books dealing with shamanism and ecstatic trance (e.g. *The Power of Ecstatic Trance: Practices for Healing, Spiritual Growth, and Accessing the Universal Mind* (Brink, 2013)). The discussion of Felicitas Goodman's history is helpful and the origins of the four states for trance inducement are detailed: open mind and relaxed body, access to a sacred space, a meditative technique (counting breaths), and rhythmic stimulation of the nervous system through rattling or drumming.

Chapter 7 discusses the mechanism for ecstatic soul retrieval and the use of analytic hypnotherapy through ritual postures. The case study of Patricia and Chuck in terms of the follow-ups is helpful.

Chapter 8 discusses the universal mind. The connection to the growing expansion of quantum physics into the social sciences is initially discussed. The discussion of the morphic field in terms of quantum physics is enticing. I love this quote by Nicholas on page 107.

> We have lost this ability to access the spirit world because during this last 2500 years of the era of rational consciousness we have limited our perceived world to the five senses, the senses of sight, sound, taste, smell and touch. Only as we learn to suppress this limited perception by going into an altered state of consciousness such as hypnotic or ecstatic trance can we again open ourselves to the broader morphic field, the world of the spirits, and thus regain the intuition that was so important to our ancestors.

The review of future dreams is intriguing. The double slit experiment is relevant to everyday living as we observe stimuli and react to it.

Chapter 9 discusses the evolution of consciousness, which is essentially dependent on the development of the cerebral cortex from an evolutionary view. The types of human consciousness in terms of Korten's stages (magical, imperial, socialized, cultural, and spiritual) help in understanding the etiology of the universal mind.

As you read this book, I want to reiterate that it is informative in tracing the history of cognitive behavioral therapy. In my personal opinion, the history of fields of knowledge is often lacking in current instruction modules. The concluding chapters point to the future in terms of quantum psychology and nuances on the theory of mind. The discussion of quantum physics is one of the most well-written explanations of its connections to psychology which has resulted in quantum psychology.

James M. Honeycutt, Ph.D
Distinguished Professor Emeritus, Louisiana State University

References

Allen, J. P., Marsh, P., McFarland, C., McElhaney, K. B., Land, D. J., Jodl, K. M., and Peck, S. (2002). Attachment and Autonomy as Predictors of the Development of Social Skills and Delinquency during Mid-Adolescence. *Journal of Consulting and Clinical Psychology*, 70, 56–66. Doi:10.1037//0022-006X.70.1.56.

Beck, A. T. (1972). *Depression: Causes and Treatment*. Philadelphia, PA: University of Pennsylvania Press.

Beck, A. T. (1983). Cognitive Therapy of Depression: New Perspectives. In P. J. Clayton, and J. E. Barrett (Eds.), *Treatment of Depression: Old Controversies and New Approaches* (265–290). New York, NY: Raven Press.

Beck, A. T. (2008). The Evolution of the Cognitive Model of Depression and Its Neurobiological Correlates. *American Journal of Psychiatry*, 165, 969–977. Doi:10.1176/appi.ajp.2008.08050721.

Bekker, M. H. J., and Croon, M. A. (2010). The Roles of Autonomy-Connectedness and Attachment Styles in Depression and Anxiety. *Journal of Social and Personal Relationships*, 27, 908–923. Doi:10.1177/0265407510377217.

Bernheim, H. (1887). *Suggestive Therapeutics: A Treatise on the Nature and Uses of Hypnotism* (2nd ed.). New York, NY: G. P. Putnam's Sons.

Brink, N. (2013). *The Power of Ecstatic Trance: Practices for Healing, Spiritual Growth, and Accessing the Universal Mind*. Rochester, VT: Bear & Company.

Honeycutt, J. M. (2003). *Imagined Interactions: Daydreaming about Communication*. Cresskill, NJ: Hampton.

Honeycutt, J. M. (2015). Imagined Interaction Theory: Mental Representations of Interpersonal Communication. In D. O. Braithwaite, and P. Schrodt (Eds.), *Engaging Theories in Interpersonal Communication* (2nd ed., 75–87). Thousand Oaks, CA: Sage.

Kelly, G. A. (1955). *The Psychology of Personal Constructs: Vol. 1 and 2*. New York, NY: W. W. Norton.

Rogers, C. (1965). *Client-Centered Therapy: Its Current Practice, Implications, and Theory*. Boston, MA: Houghton Mifflin.

Acknowledgements

First, I offer thanks to James Honeycutt for his continued support, his review of this book, and for writing the foreword. I appreciate his continued interest in his research into ecstatic trance. Second, I thank Martha Ruhe for her artistic ability in drawing the illustrations. Then I offer thanks to the Routledge editors that have supported me in the production of this book.

1 Constructivist vs. Objectivist Cognitive Therapy

Among the myriad models and schools of psychotherapy that have emerged over the last century plus, the one that has most recently risen to the top is Cognitive Therapy, a school of therapy that considers itself scientifically developed as evident in the number of efficacy studies that demonstrate its effectiveness. According to Aaron Beck who has led in the development of cognitive therapy, among these many schools, three schools have traditionally dominated: Neuropsychiatry, psychoanalysis, and behavior therapy. Though these schools are strikingly different, one basic assumption is "the emotionally disturbed person is victimized by concealed forces over which he has no control" (Beck, 1979, p. 2). Beck goes on to succinctly summarize his approach:

> This new approach – cognitive therapy – suggests that the individual's problems are derived largely from certain distortions of reality, based on erroneous premises and assumptions. These incorrect conceptions originate in defective learning during the person's cognitive development. Regardless of their origin, it is relatively simple to state the formula for treatment: The therapist helps a patient to unravel his distortions in thinking and to learn alternative, more realistic ways to formulate his experiences.[1]
>
> (p. 3)

In the process of learning the alternative ways of thinking, *corrective emotional experiences* are suggested to reinforce the new alternatives.

In spite of the effectiveness of cognitive therapy, an assumption I bring to this school is that there is always room for improvement, and that there is some good to be offered from the mentioned older traditional schools. Implied from this brief description of cognitive therapy are two concepts that have been depreciated or thrown out: One is the power of the concealed forces of the unconscious mind, and the other is the sustaining power of the origin of the dysfunctional conceptions. As we shall see, both of these concepts have something to offer for increasing the effectiveness of cognitive therapy.

The Automatic Thought

Beck, originally trained as a psychoanalyst, extensively used the psychoanalytic technique of free association. Once, while using free association, a patient whose presenting problem was the expression of anger, was asked what he was feeling. The patient's response was that he was feeling guilty, and then he went down an unexpected stream of associations of being wrong in his criticism and that others would not like him for being critical. Yet, unlike this patient, Beck admits that many patients are not fully aware of such unreported thoughts until they are led to focus on them. Beck calls these unreported thoughts *automatic thoughts*. From the school of psychoanalysis these *automatic thoughts* might be considered unconscious in that the patient is not fully aware of such thoughts. With this discovery, Beck proposes that a stimulus first triggers a conscious thought that in turn triggers an emotion, and that the conscious thought when dysfunctional needs to be replaced with a more functional thought.

Contrary to this belief that these automatic thoughts are conscious, there are those who contend that many of these thoughts are subconscious if not unconscious and are only brought to consciousness by some therapeutic trigger such as may arise in free association. Consider an example of an abusive husband who while abusing his wife triggers fear within Amy their daughter and a possible intermediary thought that husbands/fathers, and more generally men, are abusive and cannot be trusted. Thus, in later years, Amy finds that when she is around men she feels fear and anxiety. When Amy repeatedly heard and saw these acts of abuse, her intermediary thought that a husband/father, and men in general, are abusive and cannot be trusted eventually dropped out and the feelings of fear and anxiety were automatically and instantly triggered, i.e. in later years when in the presence of a husband or man her feeling of fear and anxiety arises so quickly that she does not have the chance to recall the potential intermediary thoughts, thus the thoughts are forgotten.

This automatic emotional response to observed acts of violence is parallel to what happens when someone is learning how to type. At first, seeing and typing the letter "d" requires the intermediary thought that the middle finger of the right hand needs to strike the key directly below it on the home row of the keyboard, but then with sufficient practice, the finger immediately types the letter without the intermediary conscious thought. As I write this sentence I found that I was unable to remember which finger of which hand is needed to type the "d" without first examining the keyboard and which finger I used to type it. The intermediary thoughts with practice have become totally unconscious.

Another possibility for Amy is that if the acts of abuse occurred before she was verbal, i.e. it occurred pre-verbally, then the acts directly trigger the emotions of fear and anxiety without an intermediary conscious thought, and when she becomes verbal, the fear and anxiety are automatic and continue to be triggered without thinking.

Though Beck admits that some patients are not fully aware of such automatic thoughts (1979, p. 31), he is unwilling to go as far as to consider such thoughts as unconscious. Yet, there are many subconscious and unconscious thoughts that influence a person's behavior, thoughts that may have been repressed because of their painful or traumatic nature, thoughts that were learned pre-verbally, thoughts that are not admitted because they come from what Carl Jung would call a person's shadow (Campbell, 1971, pp. 144–148), or possibly thoughts that have simply been forgotten after much repetition.

Some of these dysfunctional thoughts may surface when the person is led to focus on or becomes mindful of the feelings or emotions, but others may be at such depth that it would take more than the focus of attention to bring them to the conscious mind. Though *hypnosis* has not been considered a primary tool used by cognitive therapists, *focused attention* is one aspect of hypnotic trance. In fact, in 1841when hypnosis was first described, or you might say "discovered" by James Braid, he defined it as "focused attention upon an expectant dominant idea or image" (Robertson, 2013, p. 3).

The term *kindling*, borrowed from neurology, well describes the process of learning a dysfunctional thought, i.e. each episode of an emotional response to some trigger makes later episodes of the emotional response both more likely and more severe. Initially, early in life, something happens to cause the person to experience anxiety, or experience some other emotion such as depression, of feeling down or blue. As time goes by, something else happens to again trigger the emotion. As the emotion is repeatedly triggered, it becomes more easily, quickly, and frequently triggered, with the strength of the emotion growing in intensity, i.e. the feeling of anxiety may become a severe panic attack, or the feeling of depression may become a major depression. The triggers likely vary, i.e. different anxiety-provoking or depression- provoking triggers occur, such that any intermediary thoughts are not the same, and eventually the emotion occurs without thought and seems to come from out of the blue. In this process of kindling, any intermediary thoughts have dropped out. Also, the trigger or stimulus may so quickly trigger the emotion that uncovering the intermediary thought, yet replacing it with an alternative more functional thought, becomes essentially impossible. Thus, I have at times recommended the use of a medication to slow down this triggering process in order to provide the needed respite or needed time to insert or learn the new healthier intermediary thought.

With this understanding of the kindling process, uncovering a dysfunctional thought and then replacing it with a more functional thought presents a significant limitation to cognitive therapy. From my experience with dream work and especially hypnosis, there are other effective ways to access the unconscious mind for uncovering the deep dysfunctional thoughts and for replacing them with thoughts that are more functional.

Constructivist vs. Objectivist

In considering the nature of the mind, as suggested by Jean Piaget (1970), the constructivist considers the mind as active, giving meaning and order to what is experienced as reality. In contrast, the objectivist considers the mind as passive, simply gathering its content from the environment. These two contrasting concepts suggest two different approaches to psychotherapy. The objectivist is concerned with what the patient thinks and does not consider or ask the question, "*Why?*" The objectivist is most concerned with, "*What*" the person thinks. The first step for the objectivist is to discover what the patient thinks that is dysfunctional and causes the dysfunctional behavior. With this discovery, cognitive therapy then suggests a behavioral learning approach to change the dysfunctional thinking to a more functional and healthy way of thinking.

In contrast, the constructivist considers the mind as active in giving meaning and order to reality, and thus asks the question, "*Why?*" "Why does the client give this meaning to what he or she experiences as reality?" Then with the understanding of "*Why*," strategies are explored to change the way the client experiences reality.

For the purposes of this book, Beck's Cognitive Therapy will be referred to as Objectivist Cognitive Therapy. For him, asking the question "*Why?*" is not considered important. What is important is asking, "*What?*" "What is the patient's faulty or dysfunctional way of thinking?" The alternative model considers important the question "*Why?*" and the most efficient avenue to uncovering "*Why*" is through journeying into the unconscious mind, back to the source of when the faulty or dysfunctional way of thinking first took on a life of its own. This journey to the source of the dysfunctional automatic thought and developing strategies to change the client's experience of reality is designated as the Constructivist Cognitive Therapy. Yet, dwelling upon the origin of the dysfunctional thought as is done in psychoanalysis is not necessary. In psychoanalysis dwelling upon the origin is considered cathartic and healing, but with the constructivist approach, understanding the origin of the dysfunctional thought is for opening a strategic door for hypnotically finding and learning a healthier, functional way of thinking and thus does not require dwelling upon its origin.

The Journey to *Why*

In pursuit of "*Why?*," the most direct way of finding the answer is to journey into the unconscious or non-conscious mind, because the answers to *why* have generally been forgotten, repressed, or never put into word, thus they are not readily available to the conscious mind. Returning to Amy who is now 26 years old, she may have come to therapy because she realizes that she has the habit of sabotaging her relationships with men. In pursuing the *why* of this problem she soon uncovers the thought that after she has been in a relationship with a man for some time she begins to distrust his gentle love for her. This distrust of men has become a self-fulfilling prophesy in that in each relationship she pushes the man away. In pursuing *why*, we ask the question, "Why does she distrust men?"

Amy doesn't have a direct or immediate answer. We may suspect or have a hunch that she repeatedly witnessed her mother being abused by her father, but she may have been too young to describe what happened in words, and when she became verbal her response to the abuse was so quick and automatic that an intermediary thought was never put into words. Or maybe the abuse was so traumatic that she has repressed it, afraid to tell anyone for fear of bringing on further abuse. Such speculations by a therapist are not sufficient or even helpful. Amy needs to discover and re-experience for herself the source of her distrust.

The procedure of objectivist cognitive therapy is first to identify the feelings or affect that is associated with dysfunction, and then ask, "What are the thoughts that preceded the feelings or affect?" With mindful focused attention these preceding dysfunctional automatic thoughts may possibly become available if they are not too deeply imbedded in the unconscious mind, possibly "Fathers abuse mothers."

For the constructivist, to first uncover the *why* of the problem, in Amy's case her distrust of men, journeying into the unconscious mind opens the door for her to access that which she has repressed or does not remember. This access to the unconscious is attained through going into an altered state of consciousness, whether through dreams, the use of guided imagery or free association, or through hypnosis, or as we will explore later, ecstatic trance. The answer for Amy in finding the source of her distrust of men can be most directly found by using hypnotic age regression, carrying her feeling of distrust back through time to its source, a technique referred to as the *affect bridge* (Chapter 5). Dream work can also give direction in identifying the source of the feeling of distrust (Chapter 2). Teaching how such tools as dream work and hypnosis are used for journeying into the unconscious mind is the core of this book.

Amy, who eventually marries, may have waited to begin therapy until then, because when her husband is the least bit critical or disagrees with her about something, she is overtaken with panic and runs to her bedroom to place a pillow over her head. Her husband is very patient and gentle in his occasional criticism or disagreement. For the objectivist, the dysfunctional automatic thought that may have been uncovered is, "I cannot trust a man. I cannot trust my husband to always be gentle." Then her alternative more functional way of thinking may become, "My husband is very gentle and is not like other men. I can trust him." But learning this new way of thinking would not work. Why? In considering the origin of her feelings, in childhood she would run to her bedroom and hide in fear with a pillow over her head when she heard her father physically beating on her mother when they disagree about something. Now, each time her husband is the least bit critical of her or they have some difference of opinion, as gentle as he may be in expressing it, the instruction of the objectivist is for her to say to herself "My husband has shown me that he is gentle." Yet the feeling of distrusting a man comes flooding back so quickly and with such great intensity, that before she has the opportunity to bring to her conscious mind the alternative new way of thinking she is in a state of panic. The *corrective emotional experience* or the gentle presence of her husband is not effective. It might be recommended that he be part of the therapy process so that he can learn what he can do to help. His expression of frustration with his wife's panics only adds to her fear and anxiety. What could be most beneficial is if he would just hold her with a sense of relaxed confidence. Yet, the quickness of her emotional response, an example of *kindling*, makes such an intervention ineffective.

As we will see in Chapter 5, in using analytic hypnotherapy, we will find new hypnotic strategies to overcome the barriers to experiencing the *corrective emotional experience*. As different from psychoanalysis that dwells upon the past, depending upon catharsis for healing, the constructivist's approach briefly examines the origin of the dysfunctional thoughts and more direct hypnotic strategies become available to replace the dysfunctional thoughts with words that are more functional.

As mentioned above, the hypnotic technique of the *affect bridge* can offer a solution to avoid such barriers in uncovering *why* and the rapid emotional response or of deeper contradicting thoughts to "My husband has shown me he is gentle." While in a hypnotic trance the *affect bridge* (Watkins, 1971) would be used to lead Amy to carry back through time her feelings of panic, and possibly the words of her distrust for men, i.e. if she has already identified these words as her dysfunctional automatic thought. This hypnotic journey back through time can carry her to an early example of the source of her panic, and if she uncovers and is allowed to re-experience the panic she felt when she heard her father abusing or beating on her mother, this re-experiencing brings alive within her and provides her with ownership of *why* she distrusts men.

Learning the More Functional Thoughts

Again according to objectivist cognitive therapy, once the dysfunctional way of thinking is uncovered, regardless of its origin, the role of the therapist is to help the client find an alternative more realistic way of thinking. Once determined, by having the client repeat over and over this more functional way of thinking, along with *corrective emotional experiences* that reinforce the functional way of thinking, the new way of thinking will replace the dysfunctional thoughts and eventually become automatic, a behavioral approach to learning. The *corrective emotional experience* is important in providing reinforcement to the new way of thinking. For Amy, being held in a gentle and relaxed manner by her husband while she may feel a sense of panic can provide her with a *corrective emotional experience*.

The Constructivist Alternative

My contention is that if the origin of the automatic dysfunctional thought is uncovered and examined, that again there are procedures of analytic hypnotherapy and dream work that are most effective and efficient in leading clients to define the more functional ways of thinking and to assist them in making these new ways of thinking automatic.

From my experience, learning the functional ways of thinking through willpower and repetition is ineffective as long as there is a competing unconscious thought that overrides it. According to Daniel Aaroz (1985), Charles Baudouin (1977), of the New Nancy School of hypnosis in France from the 1920s, proposed what has become his famous "law of reverse effect." In Baudouin's words, translated from the French,

> When an idea imposes itself on the mind to such an extent as to give rise to a suggestion, all the conscious efforts which the subject makes in order to counteract this suggestion are not merely without the desired effect, but they actually run counter to the subject's conscious wishes and tend to intensify the suggestion.
>
> (Baudouin, 1977, p. 116)

In other words as revised by Daniel Aaroz: "Conscious effort of the *will* is useless as long as the *imagination* is adverse to that effort. It is not *will* (left-hemispheric functioning) that produces change but *imagination* (right-hemispheric functioning)" (Aaroz, 1985, p. 4).

For example, Amy has uncovered her dysfunctional way of thinking: "I cannot trust men." But with the suggestion that, "Not all men are abusive, and my husband is gentle," her conflicts and disagreements with her husband, as gentle as he may be, can quickly override this attempted new way of thinking and intensify the distrust and fear.

So what is the constructivist alternative? This alternative is found in helping Amy voice what she needs from her father and thus her husband, needs that are stated in positive terms. As these needs are voiced while she is still in trance, they become more unconscious and automatic. Yet, new *corrective emotional experiences* are needed to help in reinforcing the new ways of thinking. The *corrective emotional experiences* first occur when she speaks to her inner-father of what she needed from her father and then to become the good father figure by being what she needed from him in the way she relates to others.

Thus, as therapy progresses, Amy first begins to formulate the words of what she needed from her father, words that arise while in an altered state of consciousness.

> I need dad to be gentle and patient with mom. I need to see how a husband should treat his wife. I need you to not frighten me so, and

8 *Constructivist vs. Objectivist Therapy*

to be understanding and gentle with me, to listen for what I need, understand what I need, and be gentle in providing it.

The list of what is needed may be long, but it is important for Amy to put these needs into positive words. She may begin voicing these needs by saying, "Dad, I need you to stop abusing me," but this is meaningless, because it does not tell her what she needs, of how she needs to relate to others.

With Amy uncovering the *why* of her dysfunctional way of thinking and as she begins to find the ways to express what she needed or needs from her father, these expressions of need are spoken while in an altered state of consciousness to the *father* part of her inner self. With this new understanding of what it means to be a good, patient father, Amy is then led to explore and practice how she can be the good father figure to others in her life, children, co-workers, and friends, thus providing *corrective emotional experiences*, new behaviors that are quickly rewarded.

The Accuracy of the Words Used

In considering the automatic thoughts of people with a specific emotional disorder, the words of the automatic thoughts generally make considerable logical sense in bringing about the specific emotional disorder. For example, for the depressed patient, the words heard as insults or rejections are experienced as justified, e.g. "I am worthless because I am dumb, or because no one likes me." On the other hand, the patient with paranoid ideations assumes that other people are deliberately abusing him or out to get him. Thus, when the paranoid person hears words of insult or words of rejection he is quick to believe that an injustice has been done to him. Beck (pp. 84–89) has offered such formulas as a way to help determine the automatic thoughts of a person with a specific emotional disorder, e.g. "I feel worthless," or variations on these words, is the logical way of thinking for the person with depression. For the person with paranoid thoughts the logical language is, "I have been treated unjustly," or again other words that mean the same thing. These formulas presented by Beck are quite useful, but these formulas need to be used with caution. Most important is to identify and use the specific words offered by the client, and best of all, the words that arise from the client's unconscious mind. As Beck says (p. 36), "the words of the automatic thought are specific and discrete." For example, a patient may say, "I am worthless. No one likes me." Though the words, "I am no good and everybody hates me," might mean the same thing, if they are not the words used by the client, they may not resonate within the patient in defining his or her automatic thinking.

Fears similarly reflect specific disorders. The expression of fear of rejection, humiliation, or fears of such illnesses as heart attacks or cancer can trigger anxiety and panic attacks, while fears of specific definable situations, such as the fear of dogs, of heights, of fire, or of being trapped in a cave or tunnel indicate specific phobias. On the other hand, fears of some remote risk or danger that may occur when the patient should have or should not have performed a specific act indicate an obsession-compulsion. Listening to a client's specific words in expressing fear can define a specific emotional disorder, open the door to understanding the automatic dysfunctional thinking, and can help in narrowing in on its specific wording of the dysfunctional thinking. But again, identifying the client's specific wording of the dysfunctional thinking is most important.

Understanding why it is important to use the specific wording used by a client becomes clear when one understands the use of the *yes-set* to induce trance for journeying into the unconscious mind to uncover the automatic thoughts that have been lost or forgotten. Accessing the unconscious mind is facilitated by what Milton Erickson calls the *yes-set*. The royal road into the unconscious mind is through an altered state of consciousness, whether through dreams, hypnosis, or the use of imagination, and experiencing the *yes-set* is important in inducing the altered state of consciousness. What is the *yes-set*? It is the mental set of answering "yes." The words used by the therapist need to be selected with the assurance that the client will answer, "yes, that's correct." The client's answer may be verbal or non-verbal, but to be trance inducing the answer needs to be "yes." Using the client's own words most likely assures the *yes-set*. Diverging from or using variations of these words may surprise or shock the client such that he or she comes out of the altered state of consciousness. The importance of this careful selection of words is a significant diversion from the objectivist cognitive therapy model, but it can be most effective in helping the client overcome the presenting emotional disorder.

For example, Amy used the words, "When I heard dad beating on mom, I would run to my bedroom and put a pillow over my head," thus Amy resonated with the phrase "your dad beating on mom." Reflecting back that her father was abusive, or he abused your mom, did not resonate with her in the same way and would have possibly brought her out of trance. Reflecting back her own specific words is much more effective in inducing trance.

The Metaphoric Language of the Unconscious Mind

The language of the unconscious mind is not necessarily logical and linear, but important meaning is imbedded in this language. This metaphoric language is most evident in nighttime dreams but is equally found in other trance experiences. This language, when non-linear, can be considered time-free or place-free, e.g. often in dreams I may see myself as an adult, but the setting and the time of the dream may be in my childhood home and the others in my dream may be from my childhood years. This language is different from the conscious thoughts as portrayed in cognitive therapy and requires new techniques or ways of using it in the therapy setting. Sometimes it may be translated into a more linear conscious way of thinking that remains relevant to the client, but at other times the therapist needs to go with the flow of the metaphoric way of expression and lead the client to alternative healthier ways of thinking in this metaphoric language to help the individual overcome the dysfunctional ways of thinking.

Matte-Blanco (Rayner, 1981) proposes two hypotheses describing the nature of this metaphoric language. These hypotheses are defined by whether the logic of the statement is asymmetrical or symmetrical. Asymmetrical logic is the logic of the rational world, i.e. if A comes after B, then B does not come after A, or if A causes B, then B cannot cause A, i.e. the converse is not identical to the originally proposed relationship, they are thus logically asymmetrical relations.

On the other hand, if we say that A comes before B, as well as after B, or that A causes B and is as well caused by B, the relationship between A and B is symmetrical. With these definitions, then the two hypotheses are as follows:

- Ordinary logical thought, which is primarily scientific logic about the physical world, usually entertains propositions about asymmetrical relations.
- The unconscious, however, usually treats the converse of any relation as identical to it. It treats asymmetrical relations as symmetrical.

Thus, in considering the unconscious language in the following chapters, whether from dreams, guided imagery, imagination, free association, hypnosis, or ecstatic trance, the relationships between the elements of the unconscious experience are often symmetrical, whether with regard to time, space, or causality. Other characteristics of the language of the unconscious include:

- *Timelessness:* Sequentiality is not known, and time as we know it does not exist. For example, the past may be experienced in the present, or aspects of the present may be experienced in the childhood home of the past, are examples of timelessness within the unconscious mind.
- *Replacement of external by internal reality:* What we experience within ourselves is identical to what we experience outside of ourselves. For example, the part of the self that is seen in another person while in a state of trance is the move of an internal reality to the external. The anger of another person in my dream may unconsciously reflect my own anger.
- *Condensation:* Ideas derived from different time and different object relations are experienced as belonging to one object or idea. For example, a growling dog in a dream may reflect a critical parent as well as any criticism one may be facing in life.
- *Displacement:* The shifting of feelings and ideas from a primitive object to a less primitive one, with both objects experienced as identical within the unconscious. Using an example from the next chapter, a mother cat taking a kitten by the scruff of the neck, dragging it

away from a mud puddle, or a young child spilling a glass of milk may reflect the mess I am making with something in my life.
- *Absence of mutual contradictions:* Two things that may be contradictory in ordinary logic, in unconscious logic do not diminish each other, e.g. someone in a dream can be both alive and dead at the same time. This mutual contradiction likely reflects facing one's shadow, e.g. being extraverted as well as introverted in facing something in life in an assertive manner and at the same time withdrawing from it in apprehension.

Cognitive Therapy from a Psychoanalytic Perspective

First, according to Alan Javel (1999), the concept of automatic thoughts is parallel to Freud's concept of involuntary thoughts, but these thoughts reside in the unconscious. Second, according to Freud, symptom removal requires dealing with the issues in living that led to the symptoms. Again the cognitive-behavioral therapist in seeking *what* and ignoring the *why* ignores that which led to the symptoms. Also the language used in uncovering the dysfunctional automatic thoughts and in replacing them with the healthier ways of thinking is important. The Freudian process of *working through* is the process by which change occurs. Freud warned against the stress on theoretical speculation, of being dogmatic in making assertions and of being circular in reasoning. The "analyst will fail if he tries to talk about repression, limitation of libido, incest complex, etc. to a patient who has no words for such things in his experience" (Javel, 1999, p. 404). In contrast, at the other end of the spectrum, the use of hypnosis that relies upon the careful selections of words that creates a trance by inducing a *yes-set*, words that are generally used by and resonate with the client, is supported. Though cognitive-behavioral therapists are likely not dogmatic in making assertions, neither are they concerned with inducing the *yes-set*.

The Universal Mind Beyond

We have been examining how cognitive therapy can heal and provide resolution to the problems of life. The process of healing and problem resolution deals with what we experience consciously and unconsciously, experiences that affect our emotions and behavior. But what we experience as we journey using altered states of consciousness, whether through dreams, imagination, hypnosis, or ecstatic trance, may not always be limited to our conscious and unconscious mind. These experiences may be from something beyond the limits of our personal mind, i.e. from the universal mind. We have considered our mind, whether conscious or unconscious, as limited by the functioning of our brain, limited by the neurology of our physical or somatic self, but the universal mind is from beyond the limits of our body. As we heal and find resolution to our problems, the door to the universal mind opens to us to bring us to even higher levels of maturity.

As we will see in Chapters 8 and 9, there is considerable evidence that the altered state of trance can carry us beyond our personal mind and into a realm that is much broader than what is available to us through our mind that we think of as limited to our brain. This evidence suggests or validates a broader world, the world of the universal mind, a source of information of everything that has happened since the beginning of time, since the big bang. This universal mind has been hinted at by Karl Jung in his description of the collective unconscious, the mind that he sees as containing the archetypal stories of mythology.

Is this expanded awareness of the realm beyond our conscious and unconscious mind of any use to us? David Korten (2006, pp. 52–56) describes five stages developmental of consciousness. First is the magical consciousness of our infancy, a fantasy world in which we are protected by magical supernatural figures. This stage is followed by the imperial self-centered stage of consciousness, the stage of our early years when we seek to control the world around us. If we succeed in maturing beyond this stage, and there are those who do not, i.e. those who in their greed seek to oppress others for their own gain, we mature to a level of socialized consciousness when we become empathetic to the feelings of others and get along with those around us in our narrow world of family and friends. Attaining this stage of socialized consciousness is what has been the goal of psychotherapy and the attainment of which satisfies insurance companies. In this third stage we are seen as good citizens in our world of like-minded people.

But in the next two stages, the stages of the cultural creative and the spiritual creative, we become effective and self-actualized individuals in leading others to greater maturity and effectiveness in life. The cultural creative values the broader world of diversity, and the spiritual creative, as an evolutionary co-creator, values the great Earth with the interdependence of all life. It is through accessing the universal mind that this greater maturity of the cultural and spiritual creative becomes alive. When we open ourselves to the universal mind, we go beyond what is expected from cognitive therapy and insurance companies, and find ourselves in a new world, a world of becoming healthy elders and leaders within the world community.

Note

1 Though Beck uses the term *patient*, I generally prefer to use *client*, because it takes the term away from the medical model and puts more responsibility for resolution in the hands of the *client*.

References

Aaroz, D. (1985). *The New Hypnosis*. New York, NY: Brunner/Mazel.
Baudouin, C. (1977). *Suggestion and Auto-Suggestion*. London, UK: George Allen & Unwin, LDT.

Beck, A. T. (1979). *Cognitive Therapy and the Emotional Disorders*. New York, NY: Penguin Books.

Campbell, J. (Ed.) (1971). *The Portable Jung*. New York, NY: Viking Press.

Javel, A. F. (1999). The Freudian Antecedents of Cognitive-Behavioral Therapy. *Journal of Psychotherapy Integration*, 9(4), 397–407.

Korten, D. (2006). *The Great Turning: From Empire to Earth Community*. San Francisco, CA: Berrett-Koehler Publishing.

Piaget, J. (1970). *Psychology and Epistemology: Toward a Theory of Knowledge*. New York, NY: Viking Press.

Rayner, E. (1981). Infinite Experiences: Affects and the Characteristics of the Unconscious. *International Journal of Psychoanalysis*, 62, 403–412.

Robertson, J. (2013). *The Practice of Cognitive-Behavioural Hypnotherapy*. London, UK: Karnac Books.

Watkins, J. (1971). The Affect Bridge: A Hypnoanalytic Technique. *International Journal of Clinical and Experimental Hypnosis*, 19, 21–27.

2 Nighttime Dreams

First among the gateways to the unconscious mind are the dreams we experience in our sleep. The trance state of dreams comes to us from beyond our five senses of sight, sound, taste, touch, and smell. It comes to us from what we might consider a sixth sense and provides us with a sense of intuition if we open ourselves to them. There are those who might say that dreams are random and meaningless firing of the neurons of our brain, but for those of us who have recorded our dreams and explored their meaning, we realize that they provide us with important messages and insights from our unconscious mind and beyond.

One concern of dream researchers is that the dreams need to be recorded such that the recorded experience is as close as possible to the dream experience itself, i.e. the latent dream. Javel (1999, p. 404), in examining the psychoanalytic antecedents to cognitive-behavioral therapy, states that

> Freud notes that the report of a dream (the manifest dream) is a different thing from the actual dream (the latent dream) and that the reported dream is related to an environmental stimulus (the daytime residue). Freud urges that further verbal reports or associations to the initial dream report should be treated in an objective fashion, noting omissions, distortions, additions or corrections.

This is not as much of a concern for the constructivist who uses dreams in therapy, because any and all embellishments that occur in retelling the dream come from within the person and are as important to understanding the dream as the latent dream itself. As stated by David Feinstein, "It is not possible to make up a story that doesn't reveal something of your own inner life" (Krippner et al., 2007, p. 141).

The Nature of Dreams

From ancient times dreams have been considered magical, have been listened to and valued for giving direction to one's life. "From the archaeological records ... we are led to believe that most preliterate people valued their dreams and visions far more than we do, as most precious gifts, gifts from the universe" (Larsen and Verner, 2017, p. 6). More recently, the understanding of dreams has become the primary issue or goal of dream work, interpreting their metaphoric language in order to understand the message that the dream offers. Many procedures for interpreting dreams have been offered, but I contend that such interpretation needs to be done with caution, that much of the dream with its many layers meaning is easily lost or forgotten once we have interpreted the dream with one meaning and then set it aside.

The dream arises in the right brain, as do other creative activities such as dancing, acting, painting, and writing poetry. Interpreting the dream by forcing it into the rational left brain may limit the wide breadth of how the dream can affect a person's life. Exploring the dream through these other creative right brain activities can help to keep the dream alive. Such acts of creativity as dancing and acting out the dream can move the dream from the dreamer's cognitive mind so that it is felt bodily, thus experienced more totally within and throughout the person. Illustrating the dream with drawings can keep it alive visually. Rewriting the dream in the form of a poem can bring out the deeper feelings and other elements of the dream. Keeping a dream journal and regularly returning to the journal to reread past dreams, especially those which the person feels have been successfully interpreted and thus may have been set aside or forgotten, is important for experiencing the fuller message from the dreams. As suggested by the dream worker and Harvard professor, Deirdre Barrett,

> The emphasis is no longer exclusively on interpretation, however; the emotional and visual modes of experiencing are also valued for their own inherent expressive and motivational potential. Dreams are viewed as powerful metaphors that may get at issues quicker than a patient might otherwise know how to articulate ...
>
> (Rosner et al., 2004, p. 114)

Another caution for interpreting dreams as we will see in the chapters that lie ahead is that dreams may not come from the unconscious mind but from beyond, from the collective unconscious or the universal mind, in which case seeking to find how the dream relates to you personally is not as clearly defined or relevant. Dreams can be precognitive in predicting the future, or they may be shared mutually as evident in the research performed by Jean Campbell (2006) on mutual dreaming. Campbell's research reveals some connectedness of dreams when two or more people attempt to dream together even when they live at a distance from each other. Her basic design was to select groups of ten people, first from a work setting where some of the group knew each other. Then other groups were composed of those who volunteered after reading a newspaper article about her research.

The groups were given such instructions as to dream about where they would like to meet the other members of the group, or in your dream meet with and get acquainted with the members of your team. Another instruction was to meet with your team in your dream and see if you can describe the others on your team from your dream of meeting together. With regard to describing other members of your group (when the members did not know each other and had never met the others of the team), one group member described another group member named Tom who was about 5 feet, 10 inches tall with curly dark hair, 150–160 pounds, and 23 years old. The description accurately described the Tom in his team, except that he was 32 years old instead of 23. When instructed to dream about a place where you would like to meet your group, group members dreamed of such places as the beach, a restaurant, or at a party. Someone in the group mentioned dreaming of looking around but of knowing no one. Someone else mentioned feeling like someone was following them. Elements of the dreams seemed to demonstrate attempts to follow the instructions though the research did not lend itself to quantitative comparisons. Some of the participants though felt amazed by their "hits" or "near hits." As we will see in the chapters on hypnotic trance and ecstatic trance, when the group experiences are remembered and reported on more immediately, as is possible in hypnotic and ecstatic trance, there are many more examples of "hits" such that participants soon learn to expect such mutual experiences.

Another experience of dreams that goes beyond the unconscious is seen in the popular dream contest offered at the annual conference of the International Association for the Study of Dreams. A sealed envelope containing a picture is selected from several sealed envelopes each containing a different picture. Then after dreaming that night the contestants look at the set of pictures and by using clues from their dreams, they attempt to select the picture that they believed was the one selected the evening before. Their selection is often correct, better than by chance, again demonstrating the power of dreams to go beyond what is expected if dreams only related to the struggles and life of the individual. A winner is selected by a panel of judges who compare the content of the dreams and select the dream that is closest to the content of the picture. Numerous examples of such psi phenomena are found in the coming chapters.

Dream Interpretation

With these reasons for caution in mind, dream analysis of interpreting the metaphoric language of a dream does prove to be useful in the context of psychotherapy. How do we listen to and find understanding in the strange and often bizarre language of our dreams? If you have had the opportunity to attend one or more of the annual conferences of the International Association for the Study of Dreams, you will find that numerous ways to interpret dreams are offered. One of the simplest is to examine each element of the dream and ask the question, "What part of me does this element of the dream describe?" It can be assumed that since the dream has come from within me, that I have created the dream and that each element of the dream is a part of me. For example, I may dream of my mother and she is being critical of something I may have done. Metaphorically, in the dream I may have been a young child, and I spilt a glass of milk. I would ask, "What part of me is being critical, probably overly critical?" I could also ask, "What have I done that I am being criticized for, or what have I done in my life to make a mess?" Though the answers to these questions may take some time to arise, they will eventually arise and add meaning to the dream. The meaning that comes forth from the dream will likely provide some direct insight into my automatic dysfunctional thinking, especially if the dream occurs during the period of time that I am in therapy to overcome some emotional problem.

Consider another possible dream of a mother cat taking one of her kittens by the scruff of the neck and dragging it away from a mud puddle in which it has fallen. Again the same questions can be asked of the elements of this dream with the same answers, but the dream is somewhat further removed from what I might be experiencing in my waking life, thus suggesting that I may feel somewhat more threatened by the message of the dream. The greater the dream's distance from reality suggests a greater feeling of threat.

What is this mess I have made in spilling a glass of milk or of falling into a mud puddle? For the client, the answer is very personal and reflects something going on in his or her life. Maybe I have done something or said something that messed up an important relationship in my life, or I could have done something at work that makes a mess and puts my job in jeopardy. Usually the client will have some understanding as to what the mess is.

Both of these dream scenarios reveal common characteristics of the metaphoric language of a dream, i.e. both dreams are examples of *displacement* and are *time-free*, time-free in that "A" can come before "B," at the same time as "B" or after "B." I am a young child or a kitten, of an age that I was many years ago. The language of a dream can also be free of causality, i.e. in a dream "B" may cause "A," whereas in waking consciousness, "A" causes "B." Whereas in real life I caused the mess, in the dream it does not matter whether I spilled the milk or the milk was spilled on me, or whether I fell in the mud, or a mudslide ended up on me. In both cases I ended up in a mess.

Taking this language a step further, if I fell in the mud or spilled the milk, it was my fault and my thinking might be considered that of depression, but if it happened to me, like being caught in a mudslide, my thinking might be considered more paranoid. The rational logic of the metaphoric language of a dream or of other trance experiences often breaks down, typical of the thoughts of the unconscious mind.

Remembering and Recording Dreams

As a therapist I have frequently heard from clients that they do not dream, yet, except in rare occasions, everyone dreams and likely dreams for more than two hours throughout the night. For those who do not remember their dreams, it generally does not take long for them to begin to remember them if they go to bed at night with the intent of recording their dreams upon waking and have a journal and pen next to their bed in preparation to record the dreams. Another helpful suggestion is that upon waking to lie quietly in bed in the state of reverie between sleep and wakefulness and review what you remember of a dream, maybe just a few words, but those few words can lead to other thoughts and the dream soon emerges.

Dream Incubation

Because of the importance of dreams to our ancestors for contacting the inner source or spirits of wisdom and healing, from all around the world ritual incubation practices of various forms have been created and practiced to facilitate dreaming. Ancient cultures designated specific places, temples, sacred groves of trees, caves, sacred springs of water, where people, whether shamans or people in need of healing, would sleep in order to facilitate dreaming. Often a priest, priestess, or shaman would direct the ritual and offer words, calling upon the spirits or gods to bring upon the dreamer the needed knowledge or power of healing. Stories of the vision quests of when a youth was to become a man, of isolation in some remote spot in the woods, on a mountain top or in the desert, while fasting in preparation for the vision quest, are popular examples of dream incubation.

As told by Kelly Bulkeley (1999, p. 32), the Malaysian Senoi incorporated within their daily activities a morning gathering where they shared their dreams, a time when even the youngest children of the tribe participated. Bulkeley attributes the peaceful and harmonious nature of these people to this practice of sharing dreams.

In ancient Greece around 500 B.C.E., hundreds of incubation temples were dedicated to the god of healing, Asclepius. The pilgrims in need of healing would journey to these temples. On their journey they would likely refrain from food and sex to purify their thoughts to open their minds to healing. Once at the temple, they would be led by a priestess or priests through the incubation ritual and led inside where large marble blocks likely covered by sheepskin were to become their bed for the night. There is some indication that great non-poisonous snakes would be slithering along the floor, snakes that embodied the wisdom of Asclepius himself. It would be in such a setting that their dreams were incubated, with the temple attendants or priest whispering words of encouragement. In this profound state of waiting, dreams would arise that would be brought to the priest in the morning for further clarification.

Before I read Larsen and Verner's (2017) book that tells of these temples to Asclepius I had never heard of the use of snakes in such rituals of incubation, but from a series of experiences beginning with a dream that I had in August of 2008, this temple image with the snake became alive within me. In the nighttime dream I am sitting on a bench in a park with the other end of the bench attached to a tree. To my left is a heavyset man, a stranger, and beyond him is the tree. A large snake comes crawling up over the tree end of the bench and around the tree. Every so often along its body is a swollen section as if it had swallowed something whole. On the oval of each swelling is an elaborate mural, and there are four or five such murals of ancient Grecian scenes. I am fascinated by the murals. We both stand to look at the snake. The fat man is just sort of there, somewhat blocking my view, nothing else about him.

This series of experiences continued the next day as a hypnotic experience. We will examine the power of such hypnotic waking reveries in the next chapter. The next day I took the time to take this experience a step further in a wakeful state of reverie, using my office "dreaming chair," a special recliner in which I sit for going into a hypnotic trance state and during which I find answers to questions.

I see the snake and it is calling me to follow it. I follow it around the tree and find a marble staircase going down into the Earth. On a ledge next to a step is a brass or bronze Grecian urn. I follow the steps around to the right and come to a marble room with a large rectangular marble altar on which sits a large bronze or brass bowl with steam or a vapor rising from it. Naked except for a white diaper or loincloth, a man brings in a shovel full of red-hot stones and places them in the bowl. As he leaves I follow him through an archway into a dark room, where he disappears. I return to the altar room, and the snake is now wrapped around the base of the altar.

Then on May 4, 2009 while using ecstatic trance, trance induced with the rapid beating of a drum while sitting in the Mayan Oracle Posture (Fig. 2.1), I find that my hand becomes a swaying snake. It is just staring at me. I ask it about the nature of my ecstatic experiences. It says to wait and be patient. My arm becomes tired and I drop my elbow, and the snake loses its authority.

Then the snake becomes the snake of my nighttime dream, crawling around the base of a tree and into a hole with stairs going down into the roots of the tree with nooks along the stairs with Grecian urns in them. At the bottom is a room with a large marble altar with a bowl on it with steam or smoke rising from it. Out of a puff of steam and sitting beside the altar is the Mayan Oracle. I ask her my concern and she said to wait and be patient.

This sequence of experiences, first of dreaming, and then a hypnotic reverie, before having an ecstatic trance experience, demonstrates how each of these avenues for journeying into the unconscious mind and beyond may be used and can come together in an integrated whole. In this case the three experiences bring my attention to the ancient past in Greece and how the snake can be a provider of wisdom. This journey took me beyond my own unconscious mind and into the world of the universal mind. Journeys

Figure 2.1 Mayan Oracle.

Image from *The Power of Ecstatic Trance* by Nicholas E. Brink, PhD published by Inner Traditions International and Bear & Company, ©2013. All rights reserved. www.Innertraditions.com. Reprinted with permission of publisher.

beyond the unconscious mind and into the universal mind will be explored in Chapters 8 and 9.

In the book *The Transformational Powers of Dreaming* (Larsen and Verner, 2017, pp. 204–221), the authors describe an elaborate dream incubation retreat in which they participated that included as part of the ritual the writing of poetry in the form of haiku to describe the participant's dreams.

The Course of Dream Work in Therapy

The gestalt technique of identifying the part of self each element of the dream represents can bring meaning to the dream, bringing this meaning into the world of rational thinking to help in identifying the automatic dysfunctional way of thinking and the emotional problem that it causes. On the other hand, remaining within the context of the dream can also be most effective, since we would be working within the domain of the unconscious mind. For example, by first suggesting that the client go back into the dream, a trance state or altered state of consciousness, and then by encouraging him or her to be imaginatively creative and imagine what a young child could do to resolve the mess caused by the spilled milk, or what a kitten could do to recover from falling into a mud puddle, can offer a solution that uses the dream language that resides in the unconscious mind with its metaphoric content. For example the young child could call to the family cat to come and lick up the spilled milk, or the muddy kitten could go over to the nearby source of water, maybe a waterfall, and wash off the mud. No matter whether it was the child's or kitten's fault or whether it was something that happened to them outside of their control, by taking control and feeling this sense of control it can lift the client above the feelings of distress, whether due to depression, paranoia, or other disorder of thinking.

In the course of therapy with our Amy whose distrust of men was interfering with her relationship with her husband, one night she had a nightmare of her father beating on her mother. She woke in a sweat and was trembling. Her husband gently reached over to her and took her in his arms, and held her while she trembled, a story she related in therapy. I suggested that she go back to the end of her dream, of waking and of her husband holding her in a loving way, and focus on the feeling of gentle love coming from her husband. She soon was smiling and the rapid breathing that occurred while telling of the nightmare soon abated as she become obviously relaxed. I added, "Your husband is really there for you in his gentle way." I added the suggestion, "and you can ask him for a hug or to hold you when you begin to feel that sense of panic come over you."

The efficacy research of Krakow's *imagery rehearsal therapy* (Rosner et al., 2004, pp. 94–97) has shown that this same procedure can be effective in helping an individual with the nightmares of posttraumatic stress to alleviate the nightmares and other symptoms of PTSD. The PTSD client is asked to use his imagination to pick a solution to the problem presented in a nightmare, changing the nightmare in any way he wishes, e.g. becoming Superman or some other superhero to overcome the terrifying monster or some other terrifying experience. By returning to the nightmare and rehearsing the solution for a few minutes each day for one or possibly two nightmares that occurred during the week, the patient finds power over such nightmares by changing their outcome. This technique has proven successful in diminishing the nightmares and promoting recovery from the sleep disorder, helping the client to feel more rested during the day and allowing him to overcome other symptoms of PTSD. Though Krakow's technique is considered an example of the objectivist cognitive therapy, I contend that both returning to one's dream and using one's imagination are trance inducing experiences. They are avenues for journeying into one's unconscious mind and thus examples of a constructivist approach. Using one's imagination, like dreams, is from beyond a person's five senses and taps into the sixth sense.

This proactive approach to dream work can be very effective in helping a person move beyond some emotional problem that is being faced, but simply keeping a dream journal next to your bed and recording your dreams each morning can help in alleviating such problems, especially with the practice of reviewing your past recent dreams. A series of dreams often reveals the changes and progress in facing and overcoming some personal problem of life at an unconscious level. Deirdre Barrett (Rosner et al., 2004, pp. 113–122) examines dreams in several life situations, including bereavement, depression, trauma, and physical illness, and she finds that the series of dreams shows change over time to parallel the course of resolution to the presenting problem as they clarify unrealistic beliefs about the nature of the presenting problem.

After Amy's nightmare of her father beating her mother, and the hypnotic suggestion that she feel the gentle love of her husband, a week or two later she came to therapy with another dream. In this dream, Amy was in a disagreement with her husband about whether or not they needed to buy a new car. In reality they had fairly recently purchased a new car, but in the dream her husband wanted a new car and Amy felt they could not afford it. Her husband became quite insistent and raised his voice like sometimes happens in real life, and in the dream Amy began to panic as she would have in real life, went to the bedroom, and put the pillow over her head. But this time in the dream she got back up, went out of the room, found her husband, and asked him to come to the bedroom and hold her. He did and soon the feeling of panic went away.

Amy told this dream with a smile, a dream that showed the progress that was being made in therapy. By allowing herself to feel the gentle love of her husband her anxiety was diminishing.

Cognitive-Narrative Dream Work

Another dream work technique uses free association. Again the process of free association is trance inducing, comes from beyond the five senses, and opens a person to the sixth sense of a journey into the unconscious mind. The trance inducing nature of free association will be discussed in more detail in the next chapter. Oscar Goncalves and Joao Barbosa's *cognitive-narrative approach* (Rosner et al., 2004, pp. 125–136) is one of the more elaborate processes of dream work. The client is asked to recall the dream and is encouraged to elaborate on it in more and more detail. Next, the client is invited to explore the dream from each physical sense, and to increase and even exaggerate the emotional experience of the dream. Through this intensification experience of the dream, the client is asked to identify all the thoughts that come to mind, to free associate on these thoughts, to title and identify themes and meanings, and to relate these themes and meanings to waking life. Finally, the client is invited to project or create an alternative dream with new sensations, emotions, and implications in waking life. Thus, the dream work moves from being reactive to being proactive.

Molly came to her first session with the following dream: "I was trying something new in cooking dinner, and it turned out terrible, with a god-awful flavor. It was a squash dish and I was embarrassed to even have it near the table when Harry came home from work."

Before we begin to work on the dream, let me tell you a little about Molly, 29 years old. Molly initially did not want to enter therapy. She did not feel worthy of the expense that it would cost, but Harry saw how depressed she was and insisted. He came with her to the first session.

After high school Molly started college as was expected by her family, but she dropped out in the middle of her second semester. Her father was a college professor in political science and her mother had graduated from college. Upon dropping out she and a girlfriend took off to travel around the country. They got as far as Las Vegas, and there they ran out of money. Molly took a job cleaning rooms in a hotel-casino, but her girlfriend's parents bought a plane ticket to fly their daughter home. Molly found an apartment she could afford near the University of Nevada, Las Vegas and spent her free time sitting in a local coffee shop reading. She was a voracious reader of history and historic fiction. At the coffee shop she met Harry who was a graduate student, studying to be a pharmacist. When he graduated they moved to Pennsylvania to be near Molly's family, and Harry's family was in nearby Ohio.

In spite of the fact that she was a hotel maid, Harry saw her as being very intelligent, especially with her interest in history, though Molly reported that she has always felt dumb and like a failure.

With this background narrative, as told during the first session, Molly offered the above dream. Beginning with Goncalves and Barbosa's cognitive-narrative approach, I asked her first to elaborate on the dream. She reported that she wanted to try some Indian Ayurvedic cooking, and went shopping for some Indian spices. She learned that there were many variations of curry and she tried one, but she found the flavor very bitter and unpleasant. She felt like a failure. She thought her husband, being a pharmacist, might be interested in this Indian medicinal way of cooking.

She thought about this in real life, but never had the adventurous nerve to try it.

In considering each physical sense, taste, sound, smell, sight, and touch, I asked her about what she felt considering each sense. She mentioned first that she felt it in her stomach, a feeling of nausea, and in her eyes, she felt like crying. In telling this, I could see that she was beginning to tremble, and her breathing became shallow and rapid. She appeared quite anxious in her failed attempt to please her husband.

Then asking her to free-associate her thoughts, she began with "I'm a failure. I can do nothing right. As hard as I try, I can please no one."

I reflected, "Please no one?"

Yeah, I failed in pleasing Harry. I can please no one. I failed my father when I dropped out of college. My brother did well in college and dad was pleased, but on some occasions he told me, "You are your mother's daughter." My mother eventually graduated from college but has never done anything with her college education.

I then asked her to create an alternative dream where she succeeds.

"I thought that I might please Harry by cooking him a pleasing Ayurvedic dinner. We do enjoy going out to eat at an Indian restaurant."

"Okay, turn that dream around and imagine yourself cooking a pleasing Indian meal. Practice that new dream several times a day over this next week. Smell the Indian spices and chose those that you find pleasing." As described above, practicing this Krakow technique of redreaming the dream experience but with a positive outcome is trance inducing and brings about a parallel change in her unconscious thinking about herself.

Another dream work technique is that of focusing, something that is also important in objectivist cognitive therapy where focusing on what you are saying to yourself or thinking before the emotions arise that are elicited by your dysfunctional behavior. Again, I contend that focusing, whether used by the objectivist or the constructivist, is also a way of trance induction which will be discussed in greater detail in the next chapter. According to Eugene Gendlin (Rosner et al., 2004, p. 141) in his process of dream work, the focus is on *the bodily felt sense* that arises from the dream situation. In order for this experience of bodily awareness with regard to dreams to occur *space needs to be cleared*, i.e. the client needs to create emotional distance from the experience to avoid becoming overwhelmed by it. By focusing on this bodily felt sense, the client eventually experiences a *felt shift* in the experience. This process trusts that the body has or knows the answer to the problem.

The dream that Molly brought to the next session was one with greater emotional distance. It was of something that could have happened a dozen years earlier. "I am in college and it is final examination time." I encourage her to tell the dream in the present tense.

> All of a sudden I remember that I had registered for a course but had not attended classes after the first week or so. Now I am in a panic that I am

going to fail. It is a course on colonial history. I don't think I even bought the text book so I go to the bookstore, but since the semester is ending, they have taken this semester's books off the shelves. I then wake up drenched in sweat and find it is a relief that I was only dreaming.

I suggest to Molly: *"Focus* and stay with the feeling of panic, and see where this feeling takes you." It does not take her long. Soon she reports that she found it interesting that she went to the bookstore to find the text book on colonial history. With her love for reading history and historic fiction, she was ready to read the book. She was also surprised that she stopped going to the class, because again she thought she would have enjoyed it. Maybe she stopped because she knew that the course would have been easy for her and that other courses required or demanded more of her attention. But in any case, she lost the feeling of panic and found a new message in the dream of her love for history.

What was the nature of the change that occurred within Molly while working with this dream? In considering Rosner and Lyddon's (Rosner et al., 2004, pp. 181–190) distinction between a first and second-order of change, the first-order change is linear, surface, and uncomplicated, taking the form of adaption or adjustment. The second-order of change "alters the fundamental structure or organization of a system, i.e. it entails a restructuring of a client's personal identity and most basic assumptions about self and world." While re-examining Molly's dream of not being prepared for her final examination, she realized that the solution was for her to read the book on colonial history, something that she would enjoy, and that her interest and reading in history was something in which she excelled. This realization was a deeper restructuring of her personal identity, showing her greater self-confidence and thus a second-order change, a change that would be implanted within her unconscious.

Similarly, Molly's redreaming her Indian cooking dream but with a positive outcome brought about a second-order change, changing a basic assumptions about herself, again an increase in her self-confidence. Working with dreams in this way sidesteps the pitfall of some unconscious thought sabotaging the new way of thinking. Working in this way moves the new healthier way of thinking more directly into her unconscious mind, thus making it automatic.

The Objectivist Approach to Dream Work

Besides the book by Rosner, Lyddon, and Freeman, my search of the literature on dreams and cognitive therapy produced nine references, and all were from one issue of the *Journal of Cognitive Psychotherapy*, Vol. 16(1), and all nine have been republished in the book edited by Rosner, Lyddon, and Freeman.

According to Rachael Rosner (Brink, 2004), with regard to objectivist cognitive therapy, Beck argues that dreams are similar to automatic thoughts that follow a unique pattern specific to particular disorders, but on a verbal-visual continuum automatic thoughts are at the verbal end and dreams at the visual end. During sleep, with no external input, the cognitive pattern exerts maximum influence on dreams. Thus, Beck continued in his attempt to overcome the boundaries of the different schools of therapy with his broad-spectrum philosophy.

Also considering the objectivist approach, Harold Doweiko (Rosner et al., 2004, p. 61) suggests that since the process of dream recall and discussion takes place during the normal waking state, the cognitive "set" used by the client to remember details about the dream and to interpret the dream memories will contain "the same characteristic distortions that she or he normally uses to interpret external reality."

With regard to dreams, Arthur Freeman and Beverly White (Rosner et al., 2004, p. 85) suggest, as does Doweiko, that the objectivist "cognitive model sees the dreamer as idiosyncratic and the dream as a dramatization of the client's view of self, world, and future, subject to the same cognitive distortions as the waking state." Though there is truth in these statements, dreams come from the unconscious mind, and often have messages answering *"Why"* and not just *"What,"* thus providing a deeper avenue to providing for a change experience, sometimes in the metaphoric language of dreams. Also, while in the process of dream work I generally use the phrase, "Go back into the dream." This phrase is the beginning of leading the client back into the altered state of dreaming, and as the discussion of the dream continues, the use of the *yes-set* deepens trance, thus the dream work takes place in a state of trance rather than the waking state.

Dreams Can Reflect Therapeutic Progress

In that dreams are a dramatization of the client's view of self, world, and future, they can dramatize the progress made in therapy. This was evident in the progress seen in Amy's two dreams, first of the nightmare of her father beating on her mother, and then the dream of the conflict over buying a new car that ended with Amy asking her husband to hold her.

After Molly's two dreams, first of her failed attempt to cook for her husband an Ayurvedic dinner, and then of forgetting that she had registered for a history course that she had never attended and now it was time for the final examination, she came to a session with a third dream that showed the progress she has been making in therapy. Molly found this dream quite enjoyable: Her son Andy just came home from school and was quite anxious about a book report he had to give in school the next day. He had read the book about Daniel Boone and needed help in writing the report that he needed to read in class. Molly sat down with him and had him tell what he found interesting or liked in the story of Daniel Boone. She was impressed with what he had to say, and the way he told these stories that had them both laughing. She soon stopped him and had him write down the story the way he told it, and he did write it without much trouble. She too in her love of history enjoyed the stories of Daniel Boone and this dream reinforced this love, especially as she imparted it to her son. The dream was likely triggered by the fact that when she was cleaning a closet she found a coonskin cap that had been part of the Halloween costume that Andy wore the year before. A hunter friend of the family had made the cap for him. In the dream she put the cap on Andy as he told the stories and suggested that he take it to school to wear while giving his report.

Molly was finding much more self-confidence, especially in her interest and love of history, thus this dream showed that major progress was being made in therapy.

Lucid Dreaming

Lucid Dreaming is when a person while dreaming becomes aware that he or she is dreaming and with this awareness is able to ask questions and give direction to the dream. This questioning and direction can be quite useful in providing deeper understanding and open doors to personal growth. Dreaming lucidly is a learned skill and with practice can become quite automatic. Stephen LaBerge (1985) in his book, *Lucid Dreaming*, suggests that one way to incubate a lucid dream is to repeatedly ask the question while awake, "Am I dreaming?" By repeatedly asking this question it is likely that it will be eventually asked while dreaming, and then you can answer, "Yes, I'm dreaming," and then you are able to ask questions and give direction to the dream.

Robert Waggoner (2009) in his book on lucid dreaming, reported that after many years of lucid dreaming he asked of the dream the question, "What is behind the dream?" and "Where does the dream come from?" In response to these questions what he has experienced is a blue light. In Chapter 8 we will examine the evidence of the universal mind, the mind beyond the personal mind that is enclosed within the body. Laszlo (2007, pp. 71–72) reports on the research that this universal mind, or in his words the Akashic field, is in the form of a holographic matrix that becomes available to us while in a state of trance, a trance that suppresses our five senses. This blue light may be one way that this holographic matrix is experienced.

In one of my lucid dreams I was driving down a long incline of an interstate highway when I saw within the dream a semi had lost control and jackknifed, blocking the highway. Lucidly I asked my typical question of the dream, "What part of me is feeling out of control?" It was during the time that I was first beginning my private practice.

I purchased a triplex where one apartment became my office. I recall that for a short period of time I felt quite overwhelmed, anxious, and maybe not in control in this process of beginning my practice. From the dream I realized that I was making the right decisions and that my feelings of being out of control were exaggerated. In the dream I was in control in that I was able to stop safely when I saw the jackknifed truck.

Dreaming is the royal road to the unconscious. When we pay attention and value our dreams we find that they are an avenue that brings us to face our personal conflicts, initiating the process of healing. Our unconscious knows when we are ready to face the pain that is often associated with these conflicts and when we are prepared to initiate the process of resolution. The cognitive nature of this resolution through dream work is generally quite metaphoric, yet it can bring about new healthier behaviors or ways to face life that are reinforced through *corrective emotional experiences*. Upon facing the conflicts we find that our dreams can become signposts in the process of healing and resolution. Being able to provide direction within our dreams as in lucid dreaming can facilitate this process.

Dreaming can also take us beyond the self-centered process of conflict resolution and into the world beyond, into the world of the spirits and the universal mind. In this new world we find new creativity and direction towards greater maturation. Dreams can lead us to find solutions to problems beyond ourselves, problems that are affecting our community and the world. Dreams are the royal road to a fuller life once we open ourselves to them, appreciate them, and value them.

References

Brink, N. E. (2004). Book Review: Cognitive Therapy and Dreams, edited by Rachael I. Rosner, William J. Lyddon, and Arthur Freeman. New York, NY: Springer Publishing Company. *Imagination, Cognition and Personality, 24(2)*, 191–195.

Brink, N. (2013). *The Power of Ecstatic Trance: Practices for Healing, Spiritual Growth, and Accessing the Universal Mind*. Rochester, VT: Bear & Co.

Bulkeley, K. (1999). *Visions of the Night: Dreams, Religion and Psychology*. Albany, NY: State University of New York Press.

Campbell, J. (2006). *Group Dreaming: Dreams to the Tenth Power*. Norfolk, VA: Wordminder Press.

Javel, A. F. (1999). The Freudian Antecedents of Cognitive-Behavioral Therapy. *Journal of Psychotherapy Integration*, 9(4), 397–407.

Krippner, S., Bova, M., and Gray, L. (2007). *Healing Stories: The Use of Narrative in Counseling and Psychotherapy*. Charlottesville, VA: Puente Publications.

LaBerge, S. (1985). *Lucid Dreaming*. Los Angeles, CA: Tarcher.

Larsen, S., and Verner, T. (2017). *The Transformational Power of Dreaming: Discovering the Wishes of the Soul*. Rochester, VT: Inner Traditions.

Laszlo, E. (2007). *Science and the Akashic Field: An Integral Theory of Everything.* Rochester, VT: Inner Traditions.

Rosner, R. I., Lyddon, W. J., and Freeman, A. (Eds.) (2004). *Cognitive Therapy and Dreams.* New York, NY: Springer Publishing.

Waggoner, R. (2009). *Lucid Dreaming: Gateway to the Inner Self.* Needham, MA: Moment Point Press.

3 Spontaneous Trance

Telling Your Story

Think of the times you have talked intimately with a close friend and become lost in the conversation. What seemed like only a few minutes may have been over an hour. This distortion in your sense of time is a sign that you were in a trance or entranced. As the words flow freely in such an intimate conversation the words are coming from within you, from beyond your five senses, and as the conversation continues they come from deeper and deeper within you. This spontaneous trance I would call a common, everyday trance.

People find telling their own story quite enjoyable, telling it freely while others are listening. Telling your own story when not racing because of time limitations, or without a fear of criticism, is quite trance inducing, especially when the listener is listening actively, reflecting back elements of the narrative so the storyteller hears that the listener is not bored but enjoying the story and induces the *yes-set*. This trance inducing telling of a personal story with the therapist actively listening is the core of psychotherapy. It is during such moments that much is revealed about the person, especially those words that reveal a person's dysfunctional ways of thinking. When the words are allowed to flow automatically without hindrance, the client's unconscious mind is accessed and the automatic thoughts are revealed. Occasional words from the listener, words of reflection, along with occasional comments that offer direction to the flow of words, also add to the depth of trance. For example in the above story of Molly, when she mentioned that she could please no one, I reflected as a question, "Please no one?" This comment gave some direction to her flow of freely associated words and led her into a deeper trance. My words told her I was listening intently and interested in what she was saying. I was not bored.

The story of 40-year-old Matt and his depression at work was listened to actively, as were Molly's stories. Listening actively opened him to stories that resided in his unconscious mind and encouraged him to go deeper into these forgotten or repressed stories, stories of other incidents in his life that had also caused him to feel depression. His trance deepened with each story as he told of his depressions, stories that soon revealed a life pattern or maladaptive schema that was repeated over and over in his life.

Matt worked for the state department of transportation on the road crew, repairing roads during the summer and on snow removal during the winter. His depression was apparent as he described his lack of motivation in performing the tasks expected of him.

I reflected, "You just can't make yourself jump in and do what is expected of you at work."

With a slight nod of his head he continued,

> When the other men of the crew take the initiative in their work, I feel myself holding back. I am the last one to help. At times the other men get on my case for not helping when I am needed. Working for the state is the best paying job I have had and the benefits are great, but I am feeling that I could lose it.

His supervisor had recently made a few comments that he needed to take more initiative, but Matt continued to lack the energy or enthusiasm to follow this suggestion. Again I reflected, "You could lose this job, but you just can't make yourself do the work that is expected of you." As we will see in the next section of this chapter, with active listening, other stories surfaced that explained what was going on within him. My reflective comments told him I was listening, not bored, and not a threat to him.

Matt's story continued as he told of recent incidents, one of waiting as the other men grabbed push brooms to clean up after filling in a hole that was cut to check on a gas line that crossed the road. He waited until all the available brooms were in use and then just stood watching. I commented, "You watched the men grab the brooms, and at the end there was not one for you." I was careful in not being judgmental by suggesting that he was relieved or that he knew that there were not enough brooms to go around. Such comments could trigger feelings of guilt, guilt that would only add to the feeling of depression or failure.

Focusing

According to Beck (1979, pp. 29–38) one needs to focus on the automatic and dysfunctional thought that follows the triggering stimulus and precedes the emotion for the thought to be uncovered. Though Beck does not consider this automatic thought as coming from the unconscious mind, he does recognize that it may not be immediately available to the patient and thus it takes concentrated attention or focus for it to become conscious. I contend that focusing is an alternate state of consciousness that carries the person into the realm of the unconscious beyond the five senses.

Another example of trance induced by focused attention is the experience of confusion or disorientation that is experienced upon leaving the theater after watching an afternoon movie. As you leave the theater you may feel somewhat surprised that it is still light out and you may have momentarily forgotten where you had parked the car. Your concentrated attention in watching the movie was trance inducing. Then, on the way home, while driving along the expressway you miss the turn that takes you off the expressway because you were deep in some trance inducing thought, two examples of the common everyday trance.

Gendlin's process of focusing (Rosner et al., 2004, p. 141) as used in dream work is valuable in leading clients into a trance state while telling their stories or while using free association. Interrupting the telling of the client's story or the process of free association by asking the client to focus on one particular thought can lead the client to experience a situation with *a bodily felt sense*, experiencing it not just as a cognition in one's head but also somatically, taking the experience beyond the cognitive such that it is felt more totally throughout the client's body. Experiencing the feeling in totality in this way deepens the trance, and when it occurs can lead the person to experience a *felt shift*. A *felt shift* occurred with Molly when she realized that her deep and continued interest in history showed her that she was capable of success. In this sense, the focused attention of storytelling or free association does not only lead to uncovering lost or unconscious information but can also lead to a second-order change, a *felt shift*, in the way clients think about themselves and the world around them. The uninhibited flow of thoughts and words such as the process of storytelling and free association is trance inducing and a journey into the unconscious mind.

Free Association

Telling your own story when you know the listener is listening intently is trance inducing. With this opening a person can easily be led into free association, reporting things about what they are feeling and thinking without inhibition or worry about what the listener might think about them. This flow of thoughts is clearly trance inducing and carries the client deeper into their unconscious.

Beck recognized rightly that when a person is encouraged to free-associate that what is said may often be limited by what the person thinks the therapist wants to hear and may not include that which he does not want to reveal about himself. With this understanding Beck began to give some direction to the free association by asking what the person was feeling or the thoughts just before certain feelings of concern occurred. Though his questioning interrupted the process of free association and was a diversion from the customary process of free association, it did show the client that he was being listened to intently and that his words were not boring or open to criticism. Thus the questioning was trance inducing and carried the client deeper into trance. Though Beck discounts the value of the unconscious, he talks of both the use of free association and leading the client to focus on the thoughts that preceded a feeling. He does not consider important the trance inducing qualities of both free association and of focusing, nor that both are avenues for journeying into the unconscious mind.

Interrupting the process of free association with the instruction to focus on a particular feeling or thought again leads the client into a deeper sense of trance. As we shall see in the next chapter, in the process of a formal hypnotic induction, focusing on specific body sensations is frequently used for trance induction, e.g. "while focusing your attention on the crown of your head you will notice a tingling sensation." One *bodily felt sense* I have experienced that has carried me into a very deep trance is the feeling of sinking deeper and deeper into the chair in which I am sitting, and feeling smaller and smaller as I sink into the chair. I find that I can now call upon this felt sense at will when I seek to deepen my trance experience. Focusing in *concentrated attention* has been suggested by some practitioners of hypnosis as a definition of hypnotic trance.

Returning to the story of Matt, Matt has been working as a laborer on the road crew for the department of transportation. He came to therapy because of his depression. He was feeling very unfulfilled by his job and admitted openly that he does as little as possible on the job, mostly just standing around while the other men do the work. He knows he should be carrying his load but he just can't make himself do it. Some of the other men grumble when they have to ask him to help, and his supervisor has commented that he is last to jump in to help, but he cannot make himself take the initiative to help. He is beginning to think that his job may be in jeopardy so he came for therapy. He is married with two teenage children.

As I listened to his story I gave it some direction by asking if he has felt this way before, where he was just not motivated to work, to follow through on some job. He admitted that last winter when the weather was cold and the family was low on firewood, there were several ash trees near the house that were dead, but he could not make himself cut them and split the wood. He took the easy way out by buying a truckload of firewood. In past years he had enjoyed cutting and splitting firewood, and often thought that the wood warmed him twice, once when cutting and splitting it and then again when it was burned.

I then asked him for other examples, and he offered several. I had given his thoughts some direction and now he was associating freely, not fearing judgmental criticism. He told of another job that he soon quit, a job as a salesman where he had to make telephone calls and visit potential customers. It was a job where he was turned down more often than not, and from the beginning he felt like a failure. He quite quickly found it harder and harder to make the phone calls knowing that he would be rejected, so he quit after only two weeks on the job.

Another job was as a night watchman at a shopping mall. On this job he had a very difficult time staying awake while walking the perimeter of the mall. He was fired when his supervisor tried calling him one night and he did not answer the phone because he was sound asleep. His supervisor then found him asleep on a bench at the edge of the parking lot.

After a couple more similar stories he recalled how he felt after graduating from high school. In high school he was popular as an athlete. He played most sports in season and recalled that in running track he did quite well, often winning his event, but whether or not he won, at the end he would collapse with his hands over his face, hiding tears and sobs. It was so important for him to do his best, and the pressure to succeed would come out in tears and sobs, something that very much embarrassed him. But then after he graduated and found his first job, he soon found that he felt like a "nobody." He no longer impressed anybody and his life felt very empty. He felt like a failure, emptiness and failure that defined the pattern or schema behind his depression.

By giving his personal narrative some direction by asking about what other times he had the same feeling of depression opened the door to a more meaningful direction of free association. He was in a deep trance and deeply into his unconscious thinking, thinking of things about his life that he generally had forgotten or repressed because of their painful nature. When I asked him to focus on the feelings of his lack of motivation, of failure, of depression in telling other stories of his life, the doors to free association opened.

Imagination

I will frequently encourage a person to use their imagination. As stated by David Feinstein, "It is not possible to make up a story that doesn't reveal something of your own inner life" (Krippner et al., 2007, p. 141). A story that comes from one's imagination comes from beyond one's five senses, from the intuitive sixth sense, a story that when created is directly influenced by one's unconscious thinking. Krakow's *imagery rehearsal* is an example of the power found in the use of imagination (Rosner et al., 2004, pp. 89–109). Again, Krakow suggests that those who suffer with the nightmares of PTSD use their imagination to create a new ending to the nightmare that gives them the power to overcome the monster or power of the nightmare. With practice, returning to a dream and rehearsing a new ending to the dream can bring about resolution. Consciously going back into the story of a dream brings the person back into the dream state of consciousness, and thus the new ending to the dream is brought into the unconscious mind.

Matt, as a successful athlete in high school, was quite familiar with the power of using his imagination in rehearsing the outcome of some sporting event, e.g. imagining winning a track event and breaking his own record can work in breaking though limitations that he had imposed upon himself by his limiting way of thinking.

He had to admit that his job with the state department of transportation was the highest paying and most secure job that he has held since high school. Though to him he thought of a job as a laborer as very menial, working for the state keeping the roads in good repair and keeping them snow-free during the winter was greatly appreciated by the people of the state in spite of the complaints of having to slow down through frequent road construction sites. He too could admit to his frustration when coming upon a road construction site, but at the same time he could appreciate the need to keep the roads in good repair. In comparing the roads in his state to those in third world nations, he could be proud of what he does in keeping the roads in good repair. Leading Matt to imagine the importance of keeping the roads in good repair and recognizing his part in keeping them up was effective in bringing him out of his immediate depression and to carry his share of the load on the road crew. In reading an article in the morning newspaper about the problem of potholes in the roads in the early spring that caused so much car damage, it didn't take a lot for him to imagine this damage to tires, wheels and the car's suspension, and to see that his work in filling potholes was important and surely appreciated. As we shall see, this was a beginning, but there were other issues that needed to be faced to change how Matt saw life. As we move ahead we will see that imagination is central in much of the work of the constructivist approach to cognitive therapy.

Waking Morning Reverie

Most of you probably jump out of bed in the morning thinking of all the things you must do during the day. I spend some of my morning time in bed just thinking, very often about my dreams, possibly for as long as an hour. This time of reverie is of great importance. Staying in bed and letting my mind go where it takes me in the state of consciousness between sleep and wakefulness is probably one of the most important thing I do during the day. With my extensive experience of going into trance, this morning reverie often takes me beyond my unconscious and into the world of the universal mind, to the era of time-free transparency, to the world of the spirits (Chapters 6 and 7). Other times during the day I may retreat to my special chair for trance induction, whether a waking state of reverie or self-hypnosis, where I may seek resolution to special problems or answers to specific questions that arise during the day. Hypnosis and ecstatic trance as avenues into the universal mind are important, as we shall see in the next chapters, but my morning time of just letting my mind go in free association and in using my imagination is probably every bit as important. This is when I probably do my more creative thinking. I encourage clients to practice this time of waking reverie, record their experiences in a journal as you would your dreams, and report your insights in the next session of therapy. With these waking reverie or hypnagogic experiences, going into a state of reverie at other times during the day soon becomes equally useful or important.

Initially your thoughts will take you into your own unconscious mind, and this at times may be a little frightening if what you were experiencing was a nightmare, but my belief is that wherever your mind takes you, it unconsciously knows you are ready to go there and going there is where you find resolution to problems and where healing takes place. My mind often begins with reviewing my dreams, sometimes frightening nightmares. This fear may be what causes some people to jump out of bed without revisiting their dreams. With my regular practice of hypnosis and ecstatic trance, my reverie is often of revisiting these trance experiences. It has been my experience that opening yourself to possible resolution and healing greatly empowers you and with it you soon discover that you are going beyond your own personal unconscious and into the world beyond, the universal mind, the world of the spirits where there is much exciting to be learned as it opens itself to you. I find the best time for letting my mind go in creative thought is the first thing when I wake up, when I am still in a warm bed, and halfway into my dreams. Another time is when I happen to waken in the middle of the night and may feel somewhat anxious because I am having problems falling back asleep. Letting your mind go into such thoughts works as well as in the morning and also helps you again fall asleep. Other times during the day or when you go to bed at night may also work, but at those times it takes some practice to quiet you mind enough to let it go to where it wants to take you.

Returning to the session with Amy, when she woke from a nightmare of her father beating on her mother, her husband was there to gently hold her as she trembled. I encouraged Amy to spend a few minutes in bed after her husband gets up to go to work and review her dreams and thoughts, especially thoughts about her husband's gentle ways. After that nightmare, she had become much more sensitive to the gentleness of her husband, of their sitting together in each other's arms while watching television, and the way he would reach out and touch her as he would walk by her while she was working in the kitchen. She worked too, but much closer to home so was not so raced to leave in the morning and would get home a little before him. He would often help in the kitchen and it was a pleasant time for them to be together. When she gave herself a chance to think about these things, she felt much closer to him with a real sense of the warmth of his love, a big part of the healing process.

Self-Hypnosis

Once a person has experienced induced hypnotic trance and recognizes the value in the trance experience, going into a trance state becomes quite easy, especially if a particular place is set aside to practice self-hypnosis. I have a particular chair that I use for self-hypnosis and I find myself quickly in trance whenever I sit in that recliner. I use it frequently whether to revisit some dream or trance experience or in seeking an answer to a particular question or concern that I may have at the moment. I use the chair regularly before a client arrives for a session to review what has occurred or has been said in previous sessions. This review brings the client alive within me and gives me some direction as to where we might go in the session, though I avoid having preconceived ideas of where we must go. I feel more aligned with the client with this review. Similarly, what arises in a therapy session often provides suggestions as to what the client might seek in a self-hypnosis session in between therapy sessions, possibly to just review the trance experience that occurred in the session, thus keeping it alive within.

Using a special chair reserved for trance is trance inducing, but I have other self-hypnotic suggestions to deepen the trance experience, e.g. as mentioned above, of feeling myself sinking deeper and deeper into the chair and feeling smaller and smaller. There are many trance experiences that can be used similarly in this way to deepen trance of a self-hypnosis experience.

An example of this use of self-hypnosis was offered in the previous chapter in the second of the sequence of three trance experiences of the snake in the Grecian dream induction temple that wrapped itself around the base of the marble altar.

Amy has had several dream experiences of feeling the gentle loving embrace of her husband, and his gentle love is becoming more real to her. With this progress I strongly suggested that she identify a special place at home for her to practice self-hypnosis and regularly go there and return to feeling the warm, loving embrace from her husband. At the next session she reported that she had quite faithfully gone to the soft deck chair, a double chair, on her back patio that offered her a quiet spot away from all the tasks that needed to be done in the house. She found it quite easy to feel her husband sitting next to her, holding her. On one occasion she was irritated because he had phoned at the last minute to tell her he would be home late from work and she already had dinner ready for him. In going to her deck chair, she felt his warmth and also the responsible way in which he was taking care of the family in his work, a job that was requiring him to take more and more responsibility. She was able to let go of her irritable feeling, and feel the comfort of his loving warmth.

On another occasion she reported a nighttime dream of sitting in the deck chair with him with his arms around her. She was feeling much more trust in his love for her, even though at times they may have a disagreement. Feeling this trust in her dreams and trance experiences brought it more alive at other times in her life and the feeling of love and trust was rising above or starting to interfere with her instantaneous triggered fear of men when she might experience some form of disagreement with him.

Amy generally felt appreciated at work, a clerical job, and her boss was generally supportive, though she would occasionally hear him criticize one of her co-workers who sometimes made careless mistakes in her work. Those occasions would trigger feelings of anxiety, but most recently she recognized that his criticisms of the co-worker were called for, and in recognizing that he appreciated her careful work, she was beginning to feel that she could trust him to be gentle with her too. Her feeling of the gentleness of her husband that was reinforced in her dream and trance experiences was beginning to carry over to her boss.

Guided Imagery

One of my favorite guided imagery experiences was guided by Anees Sheikh with new age music playing softly in the background. He has led this experience three or four times at the annual conference of the American Association for the Study of Mental Imagery, an association that is now part of the International Association for the Study of Dreams. This experience leads a person to face life and eventual death, and is a good example of the power of metaphor in leading a person into their unconscious mind. Each time Anees has led this experience I find that I go quickly into a deep trance, and as I write this I cannot distinguish between the guiding words offered by Anees and the way I experienced them, but I write this as I experienced them.

> I find myself walking along the sandy beach with the ocean to my left and a cliff to my right. Ahead of me I see on the cliff a large beautiful home that overlooks the ocean. This image is like I might have experienced in Malibu, California near where I once lived. I walk towards the house and then up a path along the cliff that leads to the house. I go to the door. A man comes to the door, greets me, and motions for me to come in. Beyond the beautiful entryway is a beautiful living room. We enter the living room and he motions for me to sit in a comfortable leather upholstered chair.
>
> As I sit he tells me that he is about to leave and wants me to stay in the house and care for it while he is gone. He then leaves, and I begin by exploring the house as I begin to settle in. I find the kitchen well stocked with food and I find the bedroom very comfortable. As the years pass I find myself feeling very comfortable in this house and find the ways to express myself and who I am, while making the space my own. I grow to feel part of this beautiful place, but I begin to age and feel older. As the time goes by, the house begins to age though I keep it up the best I can. Then many years later there comes the day when there is a knock on the door and I answer it. Standing before me is the man that left the house to me. He is ready to move back in and I am to leave.

The house grew to be my life, and now is the time to leave the full life I have led, a metaphor for facing my death.

We have been visiting the stories of Amy and Matt. In returning to Molly, and her continued interest in history, I began by leading her in a guided imagery experience. She was excited about a planned trip the family was going to make to Gettysburg, the Civil War site. Her older son was learning about Abraham Lincoln in school and about the Civil War. Molly had never been to Gettysburg, and neither had her husband, Harry. This impending trip set up a perfect scenario for a guided imagery journey.

I suggested to Molly that she sit back and close her eyes while listening to my story:

> A few days before you leave to visit Gettysburg, you sit down with your children and begin to tell them the story of the Civil War and of Gettysburg. You are very familiar with this story and have told me you enjoy reading about the Civil War. You tell your children about slavery, about the way some of the slaves escaped from the south and found a better life in the north, and about how the north and the south disagreed about slavery, a disagreement that leads to the Civil War. You are a good storyteller and you especially have the attention of your son Andy in telling him these stories. He seems quite interested in this history, following after his mother in this interest.
>
> On Saturday as you ride down to Gettysburg, you tell Andy more stories about the battle site. When you arrive and get out of the car you feel especially excited, because you know much of the history of this place. You start pointing to things and tell your son about them. As you begin to walk around the grounds you see a tour guide with a group of people standing around her. As you get near them and start listening to her, you hear her say something that you know is incorrect. As you continue listening one person in the group asks the guide a question and she does not seem to know the answer, but you do. You speak up to give this person the answer to his question. The guide smiles and nods to you in a sign of appreciation.
>
> As you and your family continue to walk, you stay near this group that surrounds the tour guide, and as you walk soon there is another question and the guide turns to you for the answer. You feel proud of yourself for knowing the answer and Harry gives you a big smile. You have a very enjoyable day, and Harry expresses his appreciation for how much you know about American history, as the children fall asleep in the car.

The next week in the therapy session Molly reports on their trip. It did not go quite like the guided imagery experience, but the trip was very much empowering to Molly. She did have many stories of Gettysburg to tell the family and they did meet up with a tour group. The tour guide was good though she was not always accurate in her stories. Molly did interrupt the tour group once, and in the evening when they left Gettysburg her husband mentioned how impressed he was with how much she knew about the site. She had mentioned to him about the tour guide's inaccuracies and what the correct stories were. Before they left, they stopped at the gift shop and she found a book about the families of some of the Gettysburg soldiers that she had not read, bought it, and was excited about reading it to the children. She thought her son would be interested in hearing some of these stories.

The next week in school her son told of their trip to Gettysburg and mentioned how much his mother knew about the Civil War. With this comment, the teacher asked him if his mother would be willing to come to his class and tell some stories. He asked her. Molly was excited about going, and was thinking about what stories the class would most enjoy. At the gift shop her son bought a big poster of the battle site and took it to school to show the class. Molly had found on the poster one site for a story she thought his class would enjoy. Her daughter who was a couple of years younger wanted mom to come to her class, but Molly did not think that that age of child was ready to learn about the Civil War. They had bought the daughter a coloring book of Gettysburg, and Molly had copied several pages of the coloring book for her to take to the class for each of the children to color. That evening the teacher had phoned, thanking Molly for the pages. This experience added much to her sense of self-confidence.

This broad understanding of trance and the *yes-set* with its use in everyday life can open us to a new way of relating to each other in greater peace and harmony. In listening to others, even though we may disagree with their viewpoints, listening with an open mind, reflecting what they say with the affirming *yes-set*, can bring people together. We may learn something of the other person's beliefs and the other person when feeling affirmed is more open to modifying his or her beliefs. Using the *yes-set* is a tool of the effective salesman. There are those who believe that the hypnotized person can be controlled through hypnotic trance, but this is far from the truth when we understand the nature of the *yes-set*.

References

Beck, A. (1979). *Cognitive Therapy and the Emotional Disorders*. New York, NY: Meridian Books.

Krippner, S., Bova, M., and Gray, L. (2007). *Healing Stories: The Use of Narrative in Counseling and Psychotherapy*. Charlottesville, VA: Puente Publications.

Rosner, R. I., Lyddon, W. J., and Freeman, A. (Eds.) (2004). *Cognitive Therapy and Dreams*. New York, NY: Springer Publishing.

4 Hypnosis as an Avenue into the Unconscious

The Nature of Hypnosis

Hypnosis is difficult to define. One common definition, an altered state of conscious, is quite inadequate. Experiencing hypnotic trance may be the only way to understand or recognize it. When someone is first introduced to hypnotic trance, whether as a subject of trance, or when first learning about hypnotic trance, common everyday experiences of trance are often described. Three everyday experiences as mentioned in the previous chapter come to mind: The experience of driving down a Freeway deep in thought such that you miss your turn off; watching a movie in a theater and when it is over, feeling disoriented as you leave the theater, being surprised that it is still light outside, and feeling confused about where the car is parked; and third, having an intimate conversation with a friend and what seemed like only a few minutes was over an hour. The confusion and disorientation that follows a trance experience is a sign that you were in a deep trance. Deep concentration or being in such deep thought that you are unaware of what is going on around you is being in trance.

In the psychotherapy setting, even though you may not have been trained in using hypnosis, clients and even the therapist often experience such disorientation, feeling that the session was much shorter than 50 minutes. This disorientation is a sign of a good and intense therapy session, a sign of heightened rapport. I believe that it is important for a therapist to recognize such trance experiences, know how to create them, and understand their usefulness in the therapy session.

What brings about this disorientation, this hypnotic trance? According to Milton Erickson (Erickson et al., 1976, pp. 58–59), the father of American hypnosis, *joining* the client by listening intently to the client's words, accurately reflecting back what the client is experiencing such that the client feels heard and is able to answer, "Yes, that's right, you understand" to these words of the therapist, at least in thought if not in words, creates the mental *yes-set* and is the basis of trance induction. Theodore Barber replaces the phrase *hypnotic trance* with the concept of a *hypnotic mind-set* that in the words of the cognitive-behavioral therapist can be considered a *cognitive schema* (Robertson, 2013, p. 9). More specifically, the *hypnotic mind-set* is the *yes-set*, a mind-set with heightened rapport that opens the client to the suggestions of the therapist, thus creating a state of heightened suggestibility. *Heighted suggestibility* was Hippolyte Bernheim's 1887 definition of hypnosis, another early researcher of hypnosis (Robertson, 2013, p. 3).

With the *yes-set* as a basic rule of the way that the therapist speaks, trance is quickly induced, learned, and expected in each therapy session. Going into a hypnotic trance state is a learned skill such that with practice the client more quickly and with fewer words of induction is led into the state of trance. Thus trance induction follows one of the basic rules of learning theory. As we will discuss below, some clients come to therapy expecting or requesting the use of hypnosis so that at those times a more formal trance induction procedure is used to fill the expectation of the client. This formal induction is also based upon the use of the *yes-set*. But hypnotic trance does not have to be induced formally and trance can be an effective aspect of each session, of journeying into the experiences that deeply reside within the client.

In addition to the verbal use of the *yes-set*, talking in a slow manner, following the rate of the client's breath, is another dimension of the *yes-set*, of *joining* the experience of the client at a more kinesthetic sensory level. The experienced hypnotherapist is quick to recognize the depth of relaxation, the depth of trance experienced by the client, and actually experiences the same depth of trance, thus *joins* the client more totally in the experience.

When a client tells of his hypnotic experience it is important that it is told in the present tense. The use of the present tense keeps the client in trance, keeps the experience more alive and immediate, and makes it easier to continue in trance and return to the trance experience. For the same reason the therapist also needs to keep his reflections and suggestions in the present tense, and by doing so, the client will automatically follow suit.

The *yes-set* is somewhat reminiscent of Carl Rogers' (1961) idea of the importance of reflective listening to create empathy, though Rogers does not place the high need for accuracy in the wording that reflects feelings such that the client can most certainly answer, "Yes, that is correct." On the occasion that the therapist may accidentally diverge from the *yes-set*, the divergence is quickly noted by the client's reaction of coming out of the deep trance. The divergence is experienced by the client with a sense of surprise or shock when the client had been experiencing the deep sense of rapport established with the *yes-set*.

The Formal Induction of Hypnotic Trance

Central to the formal induction for hypnotic trance is again the *yes-set*. The initial instructive words for inducing trance are often, "Close your eyes, sit back and relax." When nothing or little is known about the client, observable truisms are used to create the *yes-set*, e.g. if the client is leaning back in his chair, an initial suggestion might be, "Feel the warmth between your back and the back of the chair." If the client is wearing tight jeans, "Notice the roughness of the material of your jeans as it pass over your knees." The use of such observable truisms is the beginning of developing a *yes-set*. These truisms continue, "With each breath notice the slight movement of the cloth of you shirt against your chest. As you focus your attention on the top of your head, feel the tingling sensation." With such initial inducing comments, I would be speaking these relaxing words very slowly at the rate of the client's breathing and with frequent periods of silence.

> Notice the nine points of your feet that touch the ground, your five toes, the outside edge of your foot, the pad behind your big toe, the pad behind your little toe and your heel. Feel these nine points sending roots into the floor, drawing energy up from the ground, energy that flows into and through your body, relaxing every fiber of every muscle and every muscle of every fiber of your body. Feel this relaxation moving upwards through your body. Feel the warmth of relaxation in your calves, your knees, your thighs, your abdomen. Feel the warmth of this energy spreading through your body, your stomach, your chest, your shoulders, your neck. Feel this warmth continue to spread, from your shoulders down your arms, and from your neck up into your head, your jaw, around your mouth. Feel your teeth separate as your jaw relaxes with the warmth of relaxation, from your jaw up into your face, your nose, your eyes, your ears, and up through your forehead and the back of your head to the crown of your head.

Such a relaxation exercise is a useful beginning to the use of hypnosis in therapy. "As your body relaxes, feel new strength spreading throughout your body." With these words, the relaxation exercise also becomes an ego-strengthening or emotional strengthening exercise. These words and similar words such as these are repeated and spoken at the rate of the client's breathing.

With such relaxation and emotional strengthening clients are soon ready to begin facing the concern that brought them to therapy.

> Now recall for a moment the feelings of anxiety that brought you to therapy, your words used to describe this anxiety: The tightness in your chest, your shallow rapid breathing, your racing thoughts. Let the relaxing warmth that flows throughout your body begin to melt away this tightness, the racing thoughts. Feel your mind begin to quiet, and feel your breath move downward from your chest into your abdomen as you begin to breath in the more relaxed way, breathing from your

abdomen, from your diaphragm. Your ribs that cover your lungs are ridged, restricting your breathing when you try to breathe from your chest. The more natural way to breathe is from you diaphragm, from your abdomen. When you have the chance, watch a baby breathe. Watch her abdomen rise and fall and not her chest. Breathing from your abdomen is not restricted. It is easy and normal.

These words are just one of many ways to induce trance, and with some practice, each therapist finds his or her own words that feel the most natural and effective, but the words of observed truisms and words that create a *yes-set* are spoken slowly at the rate of the clients breathing. Such a formal trance induction, with the client sharing his or her story and the therapist reflecting back the story, creates a *yes-set* that deepens the trance that is to be used in the process of psychotherapy. The next chapter presents a model of its effective use in uncovering the *why* of the emotional problem and for creating and supporting therapeutic change. But as I mentioned above, such a formal procedure of inducing trance is not necessary. Once a therapist begins to use hypnotic trance, creating the *yes-set* becomes a habit and a part of all therapy sessions.

Another factor in hypnotic trance is that it is a learned behavior. Once the learning process begins, with each further trance experience the client more easily and quickly goes into a trance, with less and less time being spent on the induction procedure. After a few sessions of experiencing trance, such words as just, "Sit back and relax," are generally sufficient to induce trance. When a formal trance induction is not used, just coming into the privacy of the therapy room is trance inducing. Understanding this concept of hypnotic trance can benefit all therapists in their therapeutic relationships to deepen rapport and increase the effectiveness of the therapy session.

Dreaming and Hypnosis

While doing dream work and in having a person return to a dream, this return leads a person back into the dream state, but the depth of trance in returning to a dream can be increased with hypnosis, by creating the *yes-set*. Recall Molly's two dreams from Chapter 2, the dream of the disastrous Ayurvedic meal she attempted to cook, and the one of realizing at the time of final exams that she had not attended a class in colonial history for which she had registered. In both dreams the therapist can reflect back her dream experience along with changes that make the ending a positive ending. "You did not go to class all semester, but you were ready to buy the text book and read it before the final exam. You had some confidence in yourself that reading the book would be interesting and sufficient."

> In cooking the squash dish something was wrong with the spices you used. You know your husband enjoys Indian food, and you learned

something in your selection of spices. You could try another set of spices and sample them before you use them to see if you might find them more satisfying.

Such reflective and suggestive statements could help Molly go into a deeper dream state as she returns to her dream to create a new and positive ending to the dream.

Free Association, Imagination, and Hypnosis

Though Free Association may not usually be thought of as a hypnotic technique, it can easily become trance inducing with an occasional reflective *yes-set* comment with the free associations coming from deeper and deeper within the unconscious mind. While using free association, Beck's (1979, pp. 29–35) question of, "What are you feeling?" was such a deepening comment that opened a new door, communicating to the patient Beck's interest in what the patient was experiencing. If while having a client free-associate the therapist simply reflects back an occasional association, the patient will go into a deeper trance. When doing dream work with Molly I asked her to free-associate on her feeling of failure in trying to please her husband. She began with "I'm a failure. I can do nothing right. As hard as I try I can please no one." By reflecting back one or more of these comments, "I'm a failure ... I can please no one," she will go deeper into the trance nature of free-associating, with associations coming from deeper and deeper within her unconscious.

Similarly, asking a client to imagine something, a new or different ending to a hypnotic experience, or pushing himself beyond his limits in performing some athletic feat or event while experiencing it in trance, can quickly deepen the imaginative experience with the imagined experience implanting itself within the unconscious mind. Pete, a runner whose best event is the mile, has felt stuck in running. He has come close to but has not been able to beat his own best time for several races. Leading him to imagine breaking his time, of feeling a new surge of energy near the end of the mile, a surge that carries him over the finish line, can help him break his own record. Again, creating a *yes-set*, while embellishing his visualization of breaking his own record, will increase the effectiveness of his use of imagination.

> You have completed three of the four laps and you see that you are maintaining your usual speed, but on this last lap, as you make the first turn, you feel a new strength, a new surge in your running, a surge that grows with each turn. As you reach the final turn before the finish line the surge is at its peak and it feels great. You know as you cross the finish line that you have broken your own record.

Keeping the trance suggestions and reflections in the present tense also makes the trance more real at the moment.

Cognitive Therapy and Hypnosis

Irving Kirsch (1996, pp. 517–519) performed a meta-analysis on two studies that demonstrate how hypnosis enhances cognitive-behavioral therapy for weight loss. He found the mean weight loss without hypnosis was 6.00 pounds whereas with hypnosis it was 11.83 pounds. This difference shows a 97% increase in treatment efficacy. At the time of the last assessment period the mean weight loss was 6.03 pounds without the use of hypnosis and with the use of hypnosis it was 14.88 pounds, thus a 147% increase in treatment efficacy.

In an earlier study Kirsch et al. (1995) performed a meta-analysis on eighteen studies in which cognitive-behavioral therapy was supplemented by hypnosis. The populations of these eighteen studies had a range of presenting problems including pain, insomnia, hypertension, anxiety, obesity, ulcers, athletic performance, and public speaking anxiety. For this wide range of presenting problems the clients who received cognitive-behavioral therapy with hypnosis showed greater improvement over 90% of the clients who received cognitive-behavioral therapy without hypnosis. The use of hypnosis entailed a hypnotic induction along with therapeutic suggestions. Most of the hypnotic inductions included suggestions for relaxation while many of the cognitive-behavioral studies without hypnosis included relaxation training, thus relaxation may have been a confounding factor, yet the inclusion of hypnosis did provide enhancement to cognitive-behavioral therapy. The size of the effect of adding hypnosis was consistent for behavioral and self-report measures of change in all eighteen studies. The average client receiving hypnosis along with cognitive-behavior therapy benefitted more than at least 70% of the clients receiving therapy without hypnosis.

Eight of the studies, for a total of 236 clients, were of those suffering from obesity. The meta-analysis for this group of studies suggested that the inclusion of hypnosis was especially beneficial for the treatment of obesity.

Hypnotic Susceptibility

Kenneth Bowers (1982) provides two important insights into the relevance of hypnosis for cognitive-behavioral therapy. First in expounding on the concept of hypnotic ability or hypnotic susceptibility, his research indicates that, at least for certain presenting problems, those that involve vegetative and autonomic functions, hypnotic susceptibility is an important determining factor for success in therapy, whereas for disorders of habit and maladaptive behaviors, hypnotic susceptibility is of less importance in determining success. Hypnotherapists have often claimed that for the run-of-the-mill variety of neurotic problems that the depth of trance is of no great importance. Bowers (1982, p. 75) shows that the depth of trance is important for many problems and more important than the therapeutic procedure used, including cognitive-behavioral therapy. Also, "therapeutic interventions that are not explicitly hypnotic in format, but which nevertheless activate the hypnotic ability of those patients who are fortunate enough to be talented in this regard," are often more effective. For example, the indirect induction of trance without a formal trance induction but depending upon the *yes-set* and slow speech at the rate of a person's breathing as presented earlier in this chapter can be effective.

Although hypnosis has not been offered as a technique within the school of cognitive-behavioral therapy, a number of the techniques for uncovering the dysfunctional thought patterns and reinforcing the new, healthier way of thinking are hypnotic, including the teaching of relaxation exercises, the use of focusing upon one's way of thinking, and the use of free association. Again the use of the altered state of consciousness of hypnotic trance is used and the factor of a client's ability to be hypnotized is important in increasing the efficacy of this therapy.

The second insight offered by Bowers is that the expression of emotions rather than their control through the use of willpower as is assumed by cognitive-behavioral therapists is important. His argument that it may be necessary to lose control of one's emotion in order to gain control is another way to change one's thoughts, behavior, or circumstances. This is supported by Daniel Aaroz (1985, p. 4) with the law of reverse effect, i.e. conscious effort of the *will* is useless as long as the *imagination* is adverse to that effort. It is not *will* (right-hemispheric functioning) that produces change but *imagination* (left-hemispheric functioning). Bringing the emotions alive within the person, thus experiencing them left-hemispherically, may be implemented through the loss of control of the emotion.

Disorder Specific Hypnotherapy

The handbooks of hypnotherapeutic techniques such as the *Handbook of Hypnotic Suggestions and Metaphors*, edited by Corydon Hammond (1990), have typically offered specific hypnotic techniques for specific disorders. Such hypnotic techniques as systematic desensitization for phobias and relaxation exercises for anxiety are two such techniques that are regularly used in cognitive-behavioral therapy. Though the cognitive-behavioral therapist does not think of this desensitization as hypnotic, when systematic desensitization was first developed by Joseph Wolpe he originally described it as hypnotic desensitization (Wolpe, 1958). Though the typical relaxation exercises are a useful adjunct in dealing with anxiety disorders, the *why* of the anxiety needs to be addressed for the therapy to be most effective, and uncovering the *why* is most effectively done through hypnosis, specifically analytic hypnotherapy, the topic of the next chapter.

Other psychological problems such as anxiety, insomnia, and other mind/body conditions are generally quite effectively treated with the constructivist approach to cognitive therapy. Carol Ginandes (Chapman, 2006, p. 247) reports that hypnosis practitioners have clinically documented over the last two centuries that the hypnotic state, coupled with suggestions, may affect autonomic, immune and endocrine system processes that have been thought to elude voluntary alteration. These include such functions as heart rate, blood pressure, breathing, blood glucose levels, calcium metabolism, oxygen saturation, gastric secretions, muscular relaxation, electro-dermal activity, circulatory changes, and basal metabolism. Such capacities make hypnosis a viable, if not the premier, choice in the clinical mediation of stress-related disorders.

I have found that using systematic desensitization with hypnosis for phobias is generally quiet effective, likely because the *why* of a phobia is quite evident. Clients seem to easily remember the source of the fear of spiders, of snakes, or the fear of high places, often because their mother or some other important person in their life expressed the same fear, a fear that was thus learned from that important person.

Hypnosis as an adjunct to cognitive therapy also increases its effectiveness in treating insomnia. From the cognitive perspective, examining the client's sleep habits and changing these habits to those more conducive to sleep, i.e. reduce the intake of nicotine, caffeine, and other stimulants, especially near bedtime; keep a regular daytime schedule for work, rest, meals, exercise, and other daily activities; do not sleep during the day, go to bed only when sleepy and reserve the bed only for sleep; do not read, watch television, or do homework while in bed; and wake up the same time every day, regardless of the amount of sleep achieved during the night (Chapman, 2006, pp. 106–107). Cognitively, the anxiety provoked by the fear of not getting enough sleep is a major factor, and cognitive therapy can address this fear. Hypnotically, relaxation exercises to decrease such somatic functions as breathing rate, blood pressure, heart rate, and to slow the brain waves to an alpha state are all most conducive to sleep. Also, while the person is in a hypnotic trance the suggestion assuring the client to trust his or her body to know when it has had enough sleep can lessen the anxiety of fearing insufficient sleep. Other fears or deeper concerns in life that may be affecting one's sleep are effectively addressed using analytic hypnotherapy, again the topic of the next chapter.

Yet, a number of psychological disorders such as depression, obsessive-compulsive disorders, and anger management show much greater resistance to cognitive-behavioral therapy and require more depth in the therapeutic process, depth that is best facilitated with journeys into the unconscious mind using such avenues as dream work, guided imagery, analytic hypnotherapy, and ecstatic trance.

Major Depression

Many other emotional disorders are less understood, or the source of the disorder is much more complex. One of these more complex disorders is a major depression. Assen Alladin (Chapman, 2006, pp. 139–188) offers a technique or model using hypnosis as an adjunct to cognitive-behavioral therapy for major depressive disorders, using it in a very specific way. After the first clinical assessment session, the second session provides a number of first aid bandages including encouraging the client to talk about the triggers of depressive episodes and to ventilate feelings of distress, offering a plausible biological explanation in order to reduce feelings of guilt, encouraging deliberate attempts to smile and imagine funny faces, playing happy mental tapes, and practicing using positive cue-words. Following this, for the next three sessions, he uses the customary model of cognitive-behavior therapy as described by David Burns, including having the client read the first three chapters of Burns' book, *The Feeling Good Handbook* (1999), and identifying the cognitive distortions that apply from Burns' list of ten distortions. Continuing in this direction, the client is asked to monitor and record life events that trigger depression, the automatic thoughts that go along with the events and the emotions these thoughts trigger. The client is then introduced to a form that logs these events, automatic thoughts, and ensuing emotions along with the disputant thought and the consequences of these thoughts. The therapist helps the client differentiate between superficial and the deeper cognitive distortions in preparation for restructuring the deeper self-schemas.

With depression that is the end product of the *kindling* process, the triggers of a depressive episode are often not apparent or are lost, especially for an episode of a major depression that lasts for weeks. These episodes often seem to come out of the blue, thus the trigger to the episode is not available to the conscious mind.

Up to this point the procedure offered by Assen Alladin is very objective and mechanical. For the next two sessions hypnosis is then introduced which induces relaxation, reduces distraction, maximizes concentration, facilitates divergent thinking, and amplifies experiences. Hypnosis provides access to non-conscious psychological processes, specifically focusing on relaxation and other somatosensory changes that demonstrate the power of the mind and increase self-confidence in using self-hypnosis. The client is given an audiotape of a counting method for induction and deepening trance and is encouraged to use it daily with the suggestion of feeling less depressed.

Hypnosis is again used in sessions nine through twelve to help in the cognitive restructuring process. First, when sufficient trance is achieved the client is to imagine a situation that would normally cause upset and to focus on the dysfunctional thoughts, triggered emotions, and the psychosomatic and behavioral responses. With this focus, the hypnotic suggestion is made to "freeze" the dysfunctional thoughts, beliefs, and images. With the thoughts frozen, the client is led to replace them with more appropriate thoughts and images. This procedure then is repeated until the client feels certain that a change has taken place. Along with this process that is facilitated with hypnosis, hypnosis is used to expand or amplify the experience, to reduce guilt and self-blame, and to open antidepressive pathways. Because of the catastrophic thoughts and images of depression, the client needs to be trained to switch attention from negative thoughts to more positive experiences. Again, while in hypnotic trance, when suggestions are made for ways of thinking positively, the new thoughts are more quickly integrated within the client.

In session thirteen, while interacting with the environment, the client needs to practice recognizing the positive nature of interactions and switch attention away from the negative anchors. Again this process can be facilitated with hypnotic practice.

Though this cognitive-behavioral hypnotherapy approach uses hypnosis to redirect the clients thinking and reinforce the new way in relating to the environment, it is not used initially in uncovering the negative cognitions and the *whys* of such thoughts.

Michael Yapko in his book, *Treating Depression with Hypnosis: Integrating Cognitive-Behavioral and Strategic Approaches* (2001), focuses on the cognitive process, whereas the client is likely to focus on the events of his or her past as the cause of the depression. In the initial interview he is quick to identify the negative processes in the client's cognition, response, attentions, and perceptual styles of facing both the internal and external world. He offers four "erroneous styles" that help in identifying the client's negative way of thinking (Yapko, 2001, pp. 43–122). The client may jump to unproven conclusions such as "it's my fault" or "that person doesn't like me." Or, the client may dwell on the past that carries the feelings of hopelessness rather than focusing on the future and its hopefulness. The third problem is the issue of control. The client needs to become sensitive in recognizing the distinctions between what can and what cannot be controlled. The fourth consideration is to examine the client's coping style of either avoiding or denying a problem, or of wallowing in the problem through rumination rather than being action oriented.

When an erroneous style is identified, Yapko uses hypnosis to help the client *deamplify* the negative or erroneous styles of thinking and to *amplify* the alternative effective lifestyles by helping the client in making decisions in selecting the more effective choices in life. This process quite directly follows the model presented by Beck (1979), but uses hypnosis to increase a client's ability to focus, to *deamplify* the negative, and *amplify* the more effective choice.

Managing Anger

Another disorder that is frequently the focus of therapy is the management of anger. Thomas Dowd (Chapman, 2006, pp. 189–212) offers a cognitive-hypnotherapy model that is based on a Buddhist conceptualization of the Four Noble Truths:

- Life is difficult.
- Life is difficult because of attachments and desires that are inherently unsatisfying.
- There is the possibility of liberation from difficulties.
- The way to this liberation and enlightenment is by the practice of compassion, virtue, wisdom, and meditation.

The suffering in life is caused by the *three poisons: Passion, aversion, and ignorance* (Chapman, 2006, p. 196).

Dowd then describes five steps towards anger reduction:

- The first step is to take responsibility for one's anger.
- Then, become aware that anger is the result of our frustrated desires and aversions.
- Three is to understand that anger reduces the sense of danger, helplessness, and humiliation and helps secure a sense of identity and meaning.
- Four is to reflect on the questions, "What did I want that I wasn't getting?" and "What was I getting that I didn't want?"
- Five is to make a commitment not to act out anger, not to repress it, but to become aware of it and reflect on it (Chapman, 2006, p. 197).

The thoughts of these five steps arise during meditation, or in a state of hypnotic trance, an altered state where upon reflection one can gently turn one's mind away from them, to reflect on compassion, and gently turn the mind once more towards compassion.

From my experience in anger management, I find much greater resistance facing one's anger as the client presents many layers of justifications for exploding. Hypnosis though is useful in overcoming this resistance and in going through these layers from the bottom up with the use of analytic hypnotherapy as presented in the next chapter and as I demonstrate in my book, *Ecstatic Soul Retrieval: Shamanism and Psychotherapy*, in the case study of Edward (Brink, 2017, pp. 97–142). The trigger to anger is so instantaneous that there is anger through all layers from the bottom up. First facing and dealing with the results of the anger at each level opens the door to moving upward through the layers of consequences to face the anger and its ineffectiveness.

Another Hypnotherapeutic Approach to Cognitive-Behavioral Therapy

Donald Robertson (2013), a psychotherapist from the UK, in his book *The Practice of Cognitive-Behavioural Hypnotherapy* offers a model that draws upon four traditions within cognitive-behavioural therapy, and integrates them with hypnotherapy: Stress inoculation training, exposure and response prevention, problem solving therapy, and cognitive therapy, the last of which provides a way to address faulty threat appraisals and cognitive distortions (Robertson, 2013, p. 29). Though diagnosis-specific conceptualizations and treatment are part of cognitive-behavioural therapy, Robertson's procedure is more from a trans-diagnostic perspective, offering procedures more defined by the severity of the anxiety faced rather than for a specific diagnosis.

Stress Inoculation Training (SIT)

Stress inoculation training (SIT) deliberately exposes a client

> to stressors in gradual doses to build up her psychological resilience, figuratively *immunizing* or *inoculating* one's self toward more severe stress in the future. The clients are trained to cope prospectively in anticipation of future stressors, e.g. repeated exposures to traumatic memories or anticipated threats.
>
> (Robertson, 2013, p. 216)

This procedure includes training the client in such coping skills as relaxation and self-hypnosis, and like systematic desensitization, it is hypnotic. SIT is used for treating mild to moderate stress and various subclinical issues.

Exposure and Response Prevention (ERP)

Exposure and Response Prevention (ERP) is used for more severe problems of anxiety. Exposure is for reducing fear or anxiety of situations or events which "the client unrealistically and mistakenly perceives as threatening or experiences as unnecessarily anxiety-provoking ... By repeated and prolonged presentation of external objects, situations, or stimuli, or internally generated thoughts, images, or memories," the client's fear or anxiety is diminished (Robertson, 2013, p. 275). Though this procedure is again hypnotic, as is systematic desensitization, the stimulus is the antithesis of SIT. With SIT the stressor is a real stress whereas with ERP, the stressful nature of the stimulus is unrealistically or mistakenly perceived as a threat or anxiety provoking. "In essence any therapeutic intervention that seeks to suppress the expression of safety-seeking responses in the context of anxiety arousal is a form of response prevention" (Robertson, 2013, p. 292).

Problem Solving Therapy (PST)

Problem solving therapy (PST), on the other hand, offers strategic ways of coping with a wider variety of problems. PST focuses on helping clients improve their general confidence and skill when it comes to solving their own problems. Robertson (2013, p. 321) presents a four step program for problem solving:

- Defining the problem: What specifically is the problem? How is it a problem? What specifically is your goal?
- Brainstorming: What possible solution strategies and tactics can you think of?
- Decision: What are the pros and cons of your options? What will you specifically do and when?
- Action: Do it! What happened? How well did it work? What did you learn? Reward your effort! What next?

These steps keep the problem and the solution in the hands of the client with the client asking and answering these questions. The therapist offers encouragement and gives the overall direction in the solution process. Hypnotic support, most specifically self-hypnosis, is offered in the form of visualization, of visualizing the various options to help in making the decision, and to rehearse the selected option through visualization.

Cognitive Therapy

The fourth cognitive-behavioural tradition considered by Robertson is the hypnotherapeutic cognitive-therapy model. He offers many useful questions that the therapist can ask of the client. Initially he asks questions that examine the normality of the client's problem: "Do these problems happen to other people as well?" "Do similar problems occur in other contexts without causing such anxiety?" and "Were there times in the past when things like this didn't bother you?" (Robertson, 2013, p. 358).

This last question is of particular interest in considering the constructivist approach. The constructivist approach considers the client's past, at the time that the problem first occurred, with the goal of determining the *why* of why the problem started.

This approach to cognitive-behavioural therapy lays the solution to the client's problem in the hands of the client. The client first considers times when the problem does not occur, and then forms a realistic appraisal of the probability and severity of the threat of the problem occurring. Next the client is to realistically appraise his or her coping ability and the appraisal of safety signs. The client typically exhibits an automatic bias towards the perception of signs of potential threat and most likely does not attend to signs of safety from the threat. A treatment plan for cognitive interventions is then considered. This is a time for educating the client about the problem and what to expect from therapy. Through discussion, a working hypothesis is developed with its treatment rationale and the client's experimentation with the hypothesis commences. Through appraising the results of this experimentation, cognitive distortions are identified and the experimentation is modified. This self-monitoring leads to the necessary cognitive restructuring and resolution. Along the way there are numerous times that hypnotic mental imagery and hypnotic rehearsal can be used effectively in providing practice in attempting new experiments or in distancing the client from troubling aspects of the problem. Hypnosis in this case is generally self-hypnosis or de-hypnosis that consists of doing the opposite, undermining negative self-hypnosis by distancing, viewing the negative autosuggestions as mere words (Robertson, 2013, p. 416).

Whereas these four hypnotic procedures facilitate the *corrective emotional experience* for learning the healthier, functional way of thinking, as we shall now see, analytic hypnotherapy uses hypnosis in the total process of cognitive-behavioral therapy, of uncovering the dysfunctional way of thinking, identifying the more functional way of thinking, and then replacing the dysfunctional thinking with the more functional way of thinking. Analytic hypnotherapy seeks the answer to the constructivist's *why* not just to *what*.

References

Aaroz, D. (1985). *The New Hypnosis*. New York, NY: Brunner/Mazel.

Beck, A. T. (1979). *Cognitive Therapy and the Emotional Disorders*. New York, NY: Meridian Books.

Bowers, K. S. (1982). The Relevance of Hypnosis for Cognitive-Behavioral Therapy. *Clinical Psychology Review*, 2(1), 67.

Brink, N. E. (2017). *Ecstatic Soul Retrieval: Shamanism and Psychotherapy*. Rochester, VT: Bear & Co.

Burns, D. (1999). *The Feeling Good Handbook*. New York, NY: Plume Publishing.

Chapman, R. A. (2006). *The Clinical Use of Hypnosis in Cognitive Behavior Therapy: A Practitioner's Casebook*. New York, NY: Springer Publishing.

Erickson, M. H., Rossi, E. L., and Rossi, S. I. (1976). *Hypnotic Realities: The Induiction of Clinical Hypnosis and Forms of Indirect Suggestion*. New York, NY: Irvington Publishers.

Hammond, C. (1990). *Handbook of Hypnotic Suggestions and Metaphors*. New York, NY: W. W. Norton & Co.

Kirsch, I. (1996). Hypnotic Enhancement of Cognitive-Behavioral Weight Loss Treatments: Another Meta-Reanalysis. *Journal of Counseling and Clinical Psychology*, 64(3), 517–519.

Kirsch, I., Montgomery, G., and Sapirstein, G. (1995). Hypnosis as an Adjunct to Cognitive-Behavioral Psychotherapy: A Meta-Analysis. *Journal of Counseling and Clinical Psychology, 63(2)*, 214–220.

Robertson, J. (2013). *The Practice of Cognitive-Behavioural Hypnotherapy*. London, UK: Karnac Books.

Rogers, C. (1961). *On Becoming a Person*. Boston, MA: Houghton Mifflin.

Wolpe, J. (1958). *Psychotherapy by Reciprocal Inhibition*. Stanford, CA: Stanford University Press.

Yapko, M. D. (2001). *Treating Depression with Hypnosis: Integrating Cognitive-Behavioral and Strategic Approaches*. Philadelphia, PA: Brunner-Routledge.

5 Analytic Hypnotherapy

Numerous books and handbooks have been written that offer specific hypnotic strategies and techniques for treating a broad range of medical, physical, and psychological problems. One particular strategy or technique of hypnosis that follows the constructivist approach to cognitive therapy is analytic hypnotherapy. This process of hypnotherapy offers a quick way to journey into the unconscious mind to uncover the *why* of the presented emotional or behavioral problem, and from the *why* to find the best words to define the *what*, the dysfunctional/automatic thinking. With this knowledge the alternative healthier way of thinking can be directly described by the client. Then hypnotically incorporating this new way of thinking into one's life can naturally follow, thus providing the reinforcing *corrective emotional experiences*. Even though the reinforcing *corrective emotional experiences* are experiences that come from the new way of behaving, this new behavior comes about through the hypnotic process of analytic hypnotherapy, thus I refrain from calling this form of therapy cognitive-behavioral therapy in favor of cognitive therapy.

The Affect Bridge and Age Regression

The *affect bridge* has become a mainstream technique of hypnosis used to uncover the source of the present problem. This technique developed by John Watkins (1971) involves first identifying the emotion or affect that is associated with the problem and then by carrying this emotion or affect back through time using hypnotic age regression the source and the *why* of the problem is identified. Identifying the source and the *why* of the problem using the *affect bridge* is much more direct than by using the psychoanalytic technique of free association.

With psychoanalysis the problem is then resolved through the process of catharsis by repeatedly facing and dwelling upon it, but Edgar Barnett (1981), in his writings on analytic hypnotherapy, added the powerful hypnotic and cathartic suggestion, "Let your adult self go back and be with your younger self, and with all the wisdom and understanding of your adult self, help your younger self understand." This language provides the client with a greater sense of self-confidence in evaluating the source of the problem, an evaluation that provides greater understanding of the problem and facilitates the catharsis. This suggestion also recognizes that since the client has chosen this time to begin therapy that sufficient adult maturity has been attained such that the client is now prepared to face the presenting problem that has likely existed for a long time, often from childhood. The problem has likely been denied or repressed, though likely showing itself in the dysfunctionality of the client.

Beyond Catharsis

For analytic hypnotherapy to continue in following the concept of cognitive therapy I have added to this analytic hypnotherapy suggestion three more steps, steps that shorten the process of catharsis (Brink, 2002, 2017):

- The suggestion that the client identify the words for what he or she needed for the source problem to not have occurred. The problem's source may occur in any of the person's primary relationships, and it is important for the statements of what the client needed in the relationship to be stated in the positive, that is, what was needed and not what was not needed, i.e. "Dad, I need you to be more gentle," not, "Dad, I need you to not abuse me." The client while in trance, whether in the therapy session or at home using self-hypnosis, is encouraged to identify as many ways as possible for expressing what was/is needed.
- Then while still in trance the suggestion is made that these words of what was/is needed be integrated within the person, e.g. "Ask the dad within you to be gentle and patient." Thus, the client incorporates within the needed traits.
- Finally, it is suggested that the client be to others, family, friends, and work colleagues what was needed from the source of the problem. The new healthier behavior is then reinforced through hypnotic suggestions and rehearsal and further reinforced when experienced in real-life situations, thus providing *corrective emotional experiences*, e.g. the behavior is reinforced "By being the gentle and patient father figure for others."

Molly

Now consider the example of Molly. Molly came to therapy because of her lifelong feelings of failure. The presenting problems that people bring to therapy may be behavioral such as an addiction and other dysfunctional habits, physical such as pain syndromes and symptoms of anxiety such as headaches or chest tightness, or emotional such as depression or obsessive fears. With most of these problems the person is readily able to identify the feelings that the problems trigger – depression, worry, anxiety, fear, etc. The use of the *affect bridge* as developed by

John Watkins is to first define the feeling or affect that the presenting problem triggers, and then using hypnotic *age regression*, to carry this feeling or affect back through time to its source. Throughout one's life many different triggers may have caused the feeling of concern, but some early events in one's life were the initial triggers of the feeling, and it is advantageous to identify these early events that have likely been repressed or otherwise forgotten and can be thought of as now residing in the unconscious mind. Thus we begin our journey back through time to the source of Molly's feelings of inadequacy.

Molly has no problem in defining her feelings, because these feelings are what brought her to therapy, feelings of inadequacy and an inability to please others in her life. In some cases feelings might not be so readily available to the client and further analytic hypnosis work may be needed to uncover the feelings, as was earlier uncovered in Molly's dreams. But now let's consider another possible scenario. During Molly's first session of therapy her story might have been simply the feelings of failure for having dropped out of college and for the meaninglessness of her employment as a maid in a casino hotel. As she tells her story her feelings would be repeatedly reflected, thus creating a *yes-set* to initiate hypnotic trance. As her breathing rate slows and her shoulders drop as the muscles of her shoulders relax, muscles that were earlier showing the tension of defensiveness, it becomes quickly apparent that she is going into trance. The sense of dropping shoulders produces the feeling of sinking deeper into one's chair, deepening the trance experience. But after the first couple of sessions it is only necessary to suggest simply that she sit back and close her eyes as she journeys back through time to find the source of her feelings of failure and inadequacy. In her current relaxed state it is quite natural for her to sit back and close her eyes. Then the hypnotic affect bridge and age regression language continues:

> As you sit there feeling very relaxed, feel yourself sinking deeper and deeper into your chair. As you sit there, carry your feelings of inadequacy and failure with you as you begin to watch your life go by. Watch it go by, hour by hour, day by day, remembering yesterday and the day before, month by month, year by year, last year, the year before. Watch your life flow by as you carry with you the feelings of inadequacy and failure, year by year. As the years flow by you will soon begin to experience those early years, the earliest years when you first began feeling inadequate and a failure. Experience those feelings as you go back through time and soon you will come to a time early in your life when those feelings began. When you come to that time, lift the index finger of your left hand.

These words or similar words are repeated slowly at her rate of breathing, until her left index finger lifts. A finger is selected that is visible to the therapist as an ideomotor signal. When Molly's finger lifts I ask her to describe what she is experiencing.

> I am in high school. I am in my room doing my homework, but with music playing on my computer. My dad comes in and with a big sigh, turns off the music. 'How can you concentrate with that music blasting?' My dad is a college professor. He teaches political science.

"Okay, we can come back to this experience, but let's go back further in time to see what else you find." I was quiet for a couple of minutes, and then said, "Carrying with you your feelings of inadequacy and failure, as you go back further in time, something else in your life will again catch your attention. When it does, again lift your finger."

After a few moments Molly again lifts her finger, and I ask her about her experience.

> I am in elementary school and I am putting on some of mom's make up and dressing up in some of her clothes that she had given me to play with. Again dad walks through the room, shakes his head and sighs. He doesn't like what I am doing.

"Okay, with all the wisdom and understanding of your adult self go back and be with your elementary school self and help your younger self understand. Your adult self understands better than anyone else."

With this suggestion Molly reports, "All I can think of is that dad for some reason is disgusted with me. Maybe he thinks I am wasting my time. He thinks I am a failure or going to be a failure."

> Okay, go back to when you are studying with the music playing. Again, with all the wisdom and understanding of your adult self, go back and be with your high school self. Your adult self understands better than anyone else. Help your younger self understand.

As a result of the suggestion, Molly reports, "I guess dad thinks it is a waste of time to listen to that music. He thinks I can't concentrate with it playing. Again he thinks I am going to be a failure like mom."

"Like mom?"

"Yeh! Mom went to college. That's where they met, but she has never done anything with her college education. She became a housewife and cared for us children."

From these hypnotic experiences using the *affect bridge* and *age regression*, the techniques of analytic hypnotherapy, what have we learned? Apparently the *why* of Molly's feelings of inadequacy and of being a failure are due to her father's sighs and disgust for what she was doing when he thought she should be doing something more constructive, studying more intently, with greater concentration. The two events that Molly re-experienced quite clearly show the source, the *why* of the problem. The *what* of what she was thinking is less defined and of less importance, but it was probably something like, "I cannot please dad."

This was likely enough to proceed with exploring what Molly needed from her father, but she wanted to repeat the analytic process one more time. She had a premonition that there may be something in her background that was even more important. She likely could have said what that something was, but the vividness in reliving the experience in trance is important.

When again going back in time she again returned to the time she was playing dress-up in her mother's clothes when her dad passed through the room and sighed. Since this is where the trance took her I again asked her what was going on, and she reported that her mother was sitting nearby when dad sighed. After he left the room, her mother mentioned that dad was disappointed that she was a girl. He had wanted a boy who could have followed in his footsteps. This new dimension is important.

The school of analytic hypnotherapy suggests that the cathartic nature of these experiences in understanding the source of the presenting problem provides the necessary healing.

I believe that it is important to go beyond these cathartic experiences and explore what the client, in this case Molly, needed from her father. These statements of need define and provide the alternative healthier ways of thinking. Thus, a more important question to be asked by Molly is "What do I need from dad?" She could say, "I wish he was not disgusted with me," but this does not say what she needs. I suggested, "Dad, I need you to be more patient with me." Then I gave her the assignment to think of as many ways to express what she needed from him and bring them to the next session.

At first Molly was not ready to face, "I need dad to want a daughter." The feeling of rejection by him wanting a son was very painful. Yet, since she had returned to those words spoken by her mother, it was apparent that she was ready to face this issue, an issue that we needed to return to the next session.

During the next session I again suggested that she sit back and close her eyes and go back to her elementary school years when she was playing dress-up. After a few moments when I could see that she was relaxed in a fairly deep trance, I suggested, "Let you adult self speak to your inner-dad figure, what you needed from dad when you were dressing up."

> Dad, I need you to appreciate what I needed to do as a child. I need you to be patient with me when I am playing as a child. I need you to smile at me, a smile that shows me that you love me.

"Okay, good. Now go back to when you were studying with the music playing and state your needs."

> Dad, I need you to accept that teenagers love their music, and it makes me feel good, it makes studying easier. I need you to recognize how much I enjoy my music. I need you to love and want me.

This last stated need was most important in dealing with her feelings of not being wanted. I suggested that we need to take this need further.

Still in trance, Molly continued,

> Dad I need you to love and want me. I need you to appreciate what women and especially mom has to offer by being the good mother in caring for your children. Dad you love what you teach, but I need you to love the lives of your children and your wife, that these lives are more important than political science.

It was obvious that Molly had been doing a lot of thinking on this subject. She knew that this would be very difficult for him to hear, but as I suggested to her I was not expecting her to tell these things to him, but to tell them to the father figure within herself, her inner-father, in order to become the good father figure to others in her life. This is something I explained to her earlier in therapy to alleviate any potential fear that she might experience from the thought of telling her father. Thus I continued:

"Feel the good, understanding, and patient father within you grow. Feel the father within you value and appreciate your family. Feel a new growing confidence within you of being a good father to others."

I then gave her the assignment to practice being the good father with others in her life, with her husband, with friends, and any other people with whom she may have contact. These interactions provide her with the *corrective emotional experiences* that she needs to reinforce her new way of thinking. When the reinforcing experiences are described during the next therapy session, the trance nature of the therapy session with the use of the reflective *yes-set* reinforces their position in her unconscious mind. Her sense of being the loving and accepting father becomes more real to her as the strength in her relationships with others grows.

Though in this example the source of Molly's problem stemmed from her relationship with her father, the source of the problem may be found in any primary or influential relationships such as with a school teacher, coach, or a scout leader, not just a parental figure. For example challenging a young person to excel in some sporting event can have a major effect, whether positive or negative. One potential negative effect could be the fear of success and fear of failure, two fears that are the opposite sides of the same coin, fears that can cause the person to give up trying.

Dream Work and Analytic Hypnotherapy

The feelings derived from a dream could have been used in analytic hypnotherapy in the same way. Let's go back to the dream scenario of Molly. In this scenario we did not use analytic hypnotherapy during the first session, but for the first couple of sessions we listened to and began working with her two dreams. The dreams, though metaphoric, revealed the same feelings of inadequacy and failure. Using the *affect bridge* and *time regression* in the process of analytic hypnotherapy would have taken us most likely to the same high school and elementary school experiences, providing us with the same *why* for her feelings of inadequacy and failure.

Recall Molly's dream of it being the time for final exams in college and she realized that she had registered for a course in colonial history but had not attended it all semester. She describes her feeling in this dream of being one of panic. I had been using the language of the *yes-set* in this and all the previous sessions so Molly was already in a trance. I suggested, Take your feeling of panic with you as you begin a journey back through time. Carrying your panic with you, watch the days, the months, the years go by as you go back through time. As you go back through time your feeling of panic will carry you back to some specific incident early in your life. When you come to that incident, lift the index finger of your right hand to let me know you are there.

Molly soon lifts her finger, and I ask her, "What is going on?"

> Dad was going to take us to Philadelphia to see the Liberty Bell. I think I was in the fifth grade. The night before I had come home from school with an arithmetic test on which I got all the problems correct. I thought dad would be happy and he seemed happy when I showed him my grade. The next morning I got ready to go with him to Philadelphia, but when I came out of my room, he and my brother had already left. I started to cry, and mom found me crying. I thought he was taking me too, but mom told me that the trip was supposed to be a special trip for him with my brother, and he wasn't planning on taking me. I felt terrible, really hurt. I'll never forget that morning. I remembered her telling me that dad wanted a son to do special things with, and I did not feel wanted. I was only a girl and he did not believe that girls would amount to anything, the same way he felt about mom. That was so unfair. Mom has told me many times that she was sorry that she ever told me that dad wanted a boy instead of me. That was the beginning of my support for equal rights for women. It is so unfair that women get less pay for the same job done by a man. I hate it that our country is run mostly by men.

Though in her dream she was in a state of panic for having forgotten about taking a college class in colonial history, this regression experience took her to a good test score she received when in the fifth grade which she thought would please her father, yet the next morning he rejected her, causing her to feel an intense panic attack.

As we pursued what she needed from her dad, Molly came up with several statements:

> I need dad to be fair. I need dad to respect me as much as he does my brother. I need parents who do not play favorites. I need dad to show me I am special and do special things with me.

These sentences were much more to the point in dealing with Molly's feelings of inadequacy than the earlier statement we had used of, "Dad, I need you to be patient with me."

Molly has, like her parents had, a daughter who is now six years old and a son four. Being the good father figure for her two children was an important beginning. She admitted with feelings of guilt that she had been playing favorites with her children, with her daughter being her favorite. She wanted her daughter to grow up with a real sense of self-confidence. She had even told her daughter, "You can do anything if you really want to do it. You could even become President of the United States." With this, she had to admit that she had shown her son much less support. Though she tried to go to most of his little league games, she missed quite a few. She was happy that his father went to most of the games and baseball was more his thing.

As the discussion went on, she was able to say that she wished that her son would not grow up thinking that guys were better than girls, and this is an attitude that she could teach him, by treating him with respect, just as she wished for him to treat women with respect. With this new awareness she found it easy to be the good father figure to her son, a father figure that showed respect for women. She returned to the next session reporting how quickly he responded to her showing him respect by him showing her respect.

We talked about this formula of how respect begets respect, respect that she could show to others at work and in particular the men, and as a result, how they too would show her respect. The following week she reported on the effectiveness of showing men respect. She was aware of several women at work who played the role of being submissive to the men, of secretaries who were ready to do anything for their boss, and that they seemed to gain little respect from the boss. Showing a man respect is not being submissive to them, but it is recognizing them as an equal. Respect needs to be shown where respect is deserved and it will be returned, leveling the playing field.

Another thing that happened from Molly being the good father figure to others is that she became more active politically in working towards equal rights for women. She had not talked to or spent much time with her father. She still felt his distance from her, but one day she was in the evening news when she was interviewed by a news reporter who was covering a women's rights demonstration in front of the office of the local congressman. Later that evening she received a text message from her father, praising her for doing what she was doing in the campaign for women's rights. This text message produced mixed feelings. She wanted to scream at him, "What took you so long?" But she was also pleased with the feeling that maybe he was coming around in believing that women can be respected, at least if they were politically active. She was still not sure if he would respect a woman for being "just" a homemaker.

With this praise she received from her father, she was motivated to do even more. She became an organizer of demonstrations for women's rights and healthcare for women, and would take both her son and daughter to these demonstrations. Someone at one of the demonstrations suggested to her, "Why don't you run for city councilwoman." At first she just laughed, and thought that would be ridiculous with everything else she was doing in organizing, working, and being a mother and a wife. But the next morning as she was waking, the time for a morning reverie, she thought about the city council and who was on it, all men. She began to think about what she might be able to accomplish if she were on the council, to give some support to the city's Women's House for abused women and Planned Parenthood, two agencies that had essentially no support from the city. She saw herself becoming an advocate for these local agencies, and began to feel excited about running for city council.

She came to the next therapy session with these thoughts in mind and was ready for my support in this venture. She did not know where to begin, and I had little knowledge. I knew that she would need to get a petition from the county elections office and have friends and supporters sign it. I suggested that she talk to her father about running for the council, but she was not in favor of that. She thought he would just laugh at her idea, but she knew that if she took the initiative and he saw that she was serious, he would get on the bandwagon.

I offered her a guided imagery exercise about how she could go about campaigning:

> Sit back and relax. Close your eyes and imagine talking to friends. The best place to start is with those you have met in your organizing for women's rights. Let them know that you are going to run for city council and ask them to sign your petition. Ask some of your best supporters to carry a petition and get signatures to get you on the ballot. You already have a telephone and email list of those who are of like mind with you for women's rights. Probably some of them are also involved in Planned Parenthood and the Women's House. Go to those agencies, talk to the staff and maybe some of their patients or clients. Tell them what you would like to do if you get on the city council.

Ask them what they would like to see you accomplish. Brainstorm and get from them who they think would be supportive of you in running for city council. Sit down with some close friends to design your campaign flyer. In talking to people imagine yourself asking for monetary donations for printing the flyers, for yard signs, and, maybe, buttons. All people running for some office have flyers, yard signs, and buttons. In talking with people, ask for volunteers to go door-to-door or make telephone calls. Think about cross-filing, about being on both the democratic and republican ballots. Remember half the population of the city are women, both republican and democrat.

As this guided imagery exercise continued, Molly reported that she had already thought of some of what I had to say, but she had not thought of some of it too. But listening to this exercise took her into a trance and it became more real to her. She could feel the excitement building. I continued,

As the days go by and the time of the election draws near, notice all the yard signs with your name on them, and notice all the people wearing your button, many who you do not know. When you see a button on someone you do not know or a yard sign in a yard you don't recognize, go to them and thank them for their support. Get their names, telephone numbers, and email address if they are willing to give them to you to add to your list of supporters. That growing list will be very important to you as your organization grows. That's what they call grassroots organizing.

Needless to say, Molly was excited and had great support in the city, especially from the women, but also from many men. It did not take long into this campaign for her father to discover what she was doing and she had his support, and behind his support, much of the support of the college where he taught political science. Needless to say, she easily won a seat on the city council.

Her life had become so busy and effective that she no longer needed therapy for support. But a couple of years later I saw that she was running for state legislator and again won. Her father must now be very proud of her and her children are experiencing the growing strength of self-confidence in their mother, and to her daughter, the possibility of becoming President of the United States does not seem out of the question.

Thus therapy took Molly well beyond the stage of socialized consciousness of what is expected by insurance companies in resolving her feelings of inadequacy, anxiety, and depression, and to a much higher level of functioning in her relationships with others around her in becoming a cultural creative (Ray, 2000). Dream work, guided imagery, morning

Matt

Returning to the story of Matt whose depression prevents him from doing what is expected of him in his work on a road crew for the state department of transportation, he recalled that when in school he was a hero as an athlete, but since graduation he has received no praise on any of the jobs he has held.

Using the *affect bridge* of analytic hypnotherapy, while carrying his feeling of depression with him on his journey back through time, the bridge initially carries him to his first job in sales in a local sporting goods store, a job that he took upon graduating from high school. Because of his success in playing high school sports, he was somewhat famous around town and his employer thought his fame might be an asset in bringing more customers into the store, but relying upon this fame did not last long and he soon became depressed and quiet.

I then suggested that we go back further in time. He was still in trance and with these words of going further back, he continued. When his finger lifted and he began to tell what he was experiencing, he told of a football game in which the score was very close. Matt ran into the end zone to catch a pass that would have been a touchdown, but he fumbled what he thought should have been an easy catch, went to the bench depressed with his head down, and his eyes covered with tears flowing from them. He felt like he was a failure and his depression lasted for several days, affecting his energy in each practice.

Again going back further in time, he came to when he was on the track team, and was running the high hurdles. He was expected to win the event against their number one rival school, but he clipped a hurdle with his left foot and fell on his face to lose the event. Again he returned to the sidelines with his hands over his eyes, in tears, and just sat, feeling like a failure. He was again depressed for several days and felt ready to quit the team.

These two incidents showed that his problem with depression started before his high school graduation. Granted, in high school he was a school hero, but any mistake brought upon him a depression that would last for several days. He tried so hard to excel in each sport but he was not perfect. Academically he was mediocre. He was happy to get passing grades, did not put a lot of energy into studying and a poor score did not cause him to cry in depression.

I felt that we were onto something new and again had him carry his depression further back through time. This time he found himself sitting in the living room at home while his mother was just ending a phone call with her sister. This aunt had a son a couple of years older than Matt who was soon to begin college. He had been accepted into the college honors program. His cousin lived on the other side of the city and went to a different high school. He might see his cousin once every couple of months when the families would get together, but his mother and her sister talked frequently on the telephone. When they talked he would sometime hear his mother telling her sister about how well he was doing in sports, but when she got off the phone he had to listen to how well his cousin was doing academically. The cousin was taking many advanced placement classes and taking a class at the local community college.

As the discussion of this experience continued, it became more and more evident that though his mother praised his athletic skill he had to be perfect for her to compete with her sister in bragging about their sons. Though he fell in running the hurdles and fumbled an easy pass, he never heard her tell her sister about these failures. In the minds of the two sisters their sons were perfect and could never make a mistake, a fantasy role that he felt he had to live up to. Only a number of years later when both boys were adults did he discover that his cousin was a real nerd in school, had no friends, spent all his time studying, never had a girlfriend, and never married. This side of his cousin, a side that could have been seen as a serious failure, was never evident when they visited when the families got together, nor was it ever talked about when the sisters talked on the telephone. Though his own academic mediocrity might have been talked about as a failure, it never was thought of as a failure by his parents or himself, but his aunt was now expressing her disappointment that her son has never married, and she was beginning to realize that she would probably never have grandchildren.

With this new understanding it took a while for Matt to find the words that he needed to resolve his depression and his need to be perfect. Eventually he was able to say:

> Mom, I need you to be honest about what I am accomplishing in life when you talk with your sister. If you were honest in telling your sister about some of my shortcomings she might open up and tell of some of her son's shortcomings.

And to his aunt, "I am sure your son is not perfect. What are some of his problems? Life has problems, no matter how small they are, and these problems need to be voiced in order to face them to find a solution."

In the next session, Matt was again led into trance and while in trance it was suggested that these words be said to the mother and aunt within him so that the words can become part of him. With this internalization it was then suggested that he needed to imagine facing others in his life with the same words of honesty. He was quick to imagine talking to one particular man on the road crew, a man that seemed to be more mature than the others and a natural leader. What he had to say in his imagination was discussed and suggestions were made in how to make the conversation more effective. Being open about personal deficiencies opens the door to overcoming the deficiencies, and when others in your life see you as a real, humble, and honest person and not just living on the past laurels of being a high school hero, it brings you closer to family, friends, and associates.

At the next therapy session Matt reported that he had confided with honesty to this one co-worker about his depression and his struggle to work. His co-worker was together enough in his own life to show his concern and compassion, and with this expression of concern and compassion, Matt felt better, was able to pick up a shovel, and take greater initiative in his work. The word apparently spread to the other co-workers and all seemed to show their concern and compassion. Though in some situations others may not be open with such concern and compassion because the world in which we now live can be quite ugly, when Matt showed appreciation to his co-workers by showing new initiative, the compassion begot compassion. Matt's depression not only lifted, but he gained a deeper understanding of the nature of his personal growth that brought about a change in the way people related to him. This broader change and growth introduced the people with whom he worked to a world of greater diversity, diversity in how people can relate effectively to others who happen to have emotional problems. The others on the road crew could feel a new strength for having helped a person with depression rise above the depression. And as Matt rose above his depression he could also feel a new strength in thanking the others of the road crew for their understanding support. This personal growth in how he began relating to others carried him beyond letting go of his self-centered need to be a hero and beyond the developmental stage of socialized consciousness (Korten, 2006), that which would have been expected and sufficient for insurance companies. His growth has taken him beyond just being part of the narrow world of acceptance in his small group of like-minded people to become a person of greater cultural creativity who can appreciate a world of greater diversity.

References

Barnett, E. (1981). *Analytical Hypnotherapy: Principles and Practice*. London, UK: Westwood Publishing.

Brink, N. E. (2002). *Grendel and His Mother: Healing the Traumas of Childhood through Dreams, Imagery and Hypnosis*. Amityville, NY: Baywood Publishing Co.

Brink, N. E. (2017). *Ecstatic Soul Retrieval: Shamanism and Psychotherapy*. Rochester, VT: Bear & Co.

Korten, D. (2006). *The Great Turning: From Empire to Earth Community*. San Francisco, CA: Berrett-Koehler Publishing.

Ray, P. H. (2000). *The Cultural Creatives: How 50 Million People Are Changing the World*. New York, NY: Three Rivers Press.

Watkins, J. (1971). The Affect Bridge: A Hypnoanalytic Technique. *International Journal of Clinical and Experimental Hypnosis, 19*, 21–27.

6 Ecstatic Trance

The use of ecstatic trance has not been explored within the context of psychotherapy until quite recently with the publication of my most recent book, *Ecstatic Soul Retrieval: Shamanism and Psychotherapy* (2017). Research of this shamanic modality has been limited primarily to the field of anthropology and to the research of anthropologist Felicitas Goodman. The energy of shamanic or ecstatic trance is seen in the familiar images of the energetic dancing of indigenous tribes from around the world, dancing that is performed to the rapid beat of drums or other percussion instruments. Such dance celebrations, celebrating the spirits of the Earth and of the ancestors may go on for many hours with some participants, generally the shaman, falling into a deep trance. From these trance experiences much is to be learned from their calling upon the spirits, spirits that give direction to life, provide healing, answer questions, and open the door for seeing into distant places and into the future. The power offered by ecstatic trance and what can be learned from it, so valued by our hunting and gathering ancestors, has been forgotten or ignored during the current era of rational consciousness, but as we move into the new age of what Jean Gebser (1985) calls the era of time-free transparency, these trance visions will again become valued and called upon. We will hear more of this power of ecstatic trance and time-free transparency in Chapter 8, but I have found that this altered state of consciousness is exceptionally valuable in the process of healing and learning from the past as we move into the future.

Research of Felicitas Goodman

The energy of ecstatic trance is very high and different from the energy of hypnotic trance, trance that is induced through slowly spoken words, words of relaxation, quieting the mind and slowing other bodily functions. Felicitas Goodman (1990) recognized that ecstatic trance is akin to speaking in tongues as occurs in the Apostolic Church. Her research in ecstatic trance thus began with her dissertation research on the speaking in tongues in the Spanish speaking and Mayan speaking Apostolic Churches of Mexico.

This research led her to identify four necessary components for inducing the trance state that produced the speaking in tongues:

- An open mind and relaxed body, along with the expectation of a pleasurable but non-ordinary state of reality.
- A sacred space, one separate from the activities of everyday life.
- A meditative technique, such as counting one's breath, to calm the analytic mind.
- Rhythmic stimulation of the nervous system through rattling or drumming.

These four components were evident in the worship services of the Apostolic Churches with the congregation's expectation of speaking in tongues, the sacred space of the church, quieting the mind with prayer, and the rhythmic stimulation of hand clapping.

Induction of Ecstatic Trance

Goodman then designed a ritual with these four components that separated them from the context of the church. Her Earth oriented ritual begins with a discussion of what to expect from ecstatic trance and the answers to questions, then the sacred space for this ritual is designated by smudging the space and each participant with the smoke of burning herbs, and by calling the spirits of the six or seven directions. The litany I generally use for calling the spirits begins while facing the east: "Spirits of the East, of the sunrise, of spring, of birth and the beginning of life, we honor you. Please join us and bring us your wisdom." After offering these spirits a pinch of cornmeal I turn and face the south with the words: "Spirits of the South, of summer and the warmth of the middle of day, of growth of our children and our gardens, we honor you. Please join us and bring us your wisdom." With a toss of cornmeal to the south I turn to the west with the words: "Spirits of the west, of the sunset and autumn, the productive years of life and the harvest of our gardens, we honor you. Please join us and bring us your wisdom." Then after the toss of a pinch of cornmeal to the west I turn to the north with a toss of cornmeal and the words: Spirits of the north, of nighttime and winter, the spirits that come to us in our dreams, the spirits of hibernation, dormancy, and death in preparation for a new birth at spring, we honor you. Please join us and bring us your wisdom. Raising my arms to the heavens with a pinch of cornmeal I use the words: Spirits of the universe, of the stars, sun, and moon, spirits of the universe that place our Earth in its position with respect to the sun such that it can sustain life, that brings us the seasons, night, and day, and the tides of the oceans, we honor you. Please join us and bring us your wisdom. Finally I reach down towards the Earth with a pinch of cornmeal and the words: "Spirits of the Earth that sustain life through the interdependence of all things, we honor you. Please join us and bring us your wisdom."

Following this litany, the meditative technique to quiet the mind is offered that entails sitting in silence in a comfortable position while counting one's breath for five minutes. Then the stimulation of the nervous system with drumming or rattling commences and lasts for 15 minutes. The beat is approximately at a rate of 210 beats per minute.

After receiving her PhD in 1971 from Ohio State University Dr. Goodman took a position at Dennison University in Granville, Ohio, a position that lasted until 1979 when she was forced to retire at the age of 65. With her students at Dennison she experimented with this ritual and found that the students did go into a trance, though she concluded from this experimentation that the trance lacked direction or meaning.

The Body Postures

Sometime later Goodman read an article by the Canadian psychologist V. F. Emerson (1972) who, in his research with various meditative disciplines, found that different body postures had specific but different effects on such body functions as heartbeat, breathing, skin moisture, and bowel motility. With this discovery, Goodman searched ethnographic journals, books, and museums to find what she believed were the body postures used by both contemporary and ancient hunting and gathering shamans, body postures that suggested religious ritual activity. She identified approximately 50 such postures that she used in her continued research. Following the ritual that she had already developed but adding to it these body postures, she had her students at Dennison sit, stand, or lie in one of these postures while she rapidly shook her rattle or beat her drum at approximately 210 beats per minute.

With this addition of a body posture which was held by the participants for the 15 minutes of drumming or rattling, she found the direction and meaning that was initially missing without the use of these body postures. What she found is that some specific body postures elicit the sensation of bringing a healing or strengthening energy into one's body. Other postures are for divination, for seeking answers to questions, or for looking into the future. Then there are those postures that bring about the sensation of shape-shifting or a metamorphosis in becoming some animal, other living creature, or some inanimate substance or feature of the Earth. Some postures are for journeying into the under world, others for journeying in this the middle world, and some for journeying in the upper world. Then there are the postures that bring about an initiation or a death-rebirth experience. Besides these seven ecstatic trance experiences, several other postures were determined to offer a celebration experience or an experience of calling the spirits.

I was first introduced to ecstatic trance when I was president of the American Association for the Study of Mental Imagery. In the beginning stages of developing the program for our 2004 annual conference Felicitas Goodman was invited to be a keynote speaker. Because of some problems out of our control the conference did not happen, but I briefly talked with Felicitas on the telephone and read her book, *Where the Spirits Ride the Wind* (1990). I was quite impressed with the outcome of her research such that in 2007 I offered a workshop in using ecstatic trance at the annual conference of the International Association for the Study of Dreams. The mental imagery association has since become part of the dream association. The workshop was offered each of the four mornings of the conference and I had the opportunity to use eight of her ecstatic postures. Granted, the participants in the group were there because of their interest in dreams thus quite receptive to this altered state of consciousness, but I was astounded by the results that matched the results of the postures as used by Goodman. As a result I returned home to start a group using the postures, a group that at first met weekly, but now meets monthly and has continued for ten years. From the ecstatic experiences of the participants of these group sessions as well as a number of other workshops I have offered around the country, I continue to be very impressed with the power of these ecstatic postures and the power of ecstatic trance.

Also evident is that Felicitas Goodman experienced this same power in the use of the postures and ecstatic trance such that she started what is now the Cuyamungue Institute, on the Pojoaque Pueblo north of Santa Fe, New Mexico, an institute that has continued to function and grow since her death in 2005.

Healing

I estimate that I have collected close to 3000 ecstatic experiences from the participants of the groups I have led. These experiences have shown me the healing power of ecstatic trance, of helping a person overcome her depression, helping another individual clarify her own identity, helping someone overcome the emotional effects of sexual assault, and the resolutions of many other problems. I am sure that many other examples of the healing effect of ecstatic trance have not been shared with me. The healing and resolution of such problems happen without the needed direction of a psychologist. The individual's commitment to use ecstatic trance on a regular basis is sufficient. I believe that many of these changes happen without my awareness as the group leader, as the ecstatic postures take these individuals beyond just their conscious mind to include the entire body in the process of change. When the mind and body work together the unconscious knows what the person needs to change and to promote growth. With this growth and the resolution of conflict and other concerns, the person is freed to go beyond the self-centeredness of these conflicts and concerns

Ecstatic Trance 73

to become a self-actualized or a cultural creative person, and an important influence in the lives of others.

One of the very first experiences of healing that was shared was Maria's who found an end to her smoking, a great example of the power of metaphor, the language of the unconscious. She used the Nupe Divination Posture (Fig 6.1) which was found in Lucy Mair's book *Witchcraft* (1969) and is a picture of a Nupe shaman of sub-Sahara, Africa.

Figure 6.1 Nupe Diviner.

Image from *The Power of Ecstatic Trance* by Nicholas E. Brink, PhD published by Inner Traditions International and Bear & Company, ©2013. All rights reserved. www.Innertraditions.com Reprinted with permission of publisher.

This posture brought Maria the following experience as first reported in *The Power of Ecstatic Trance*:

> 10/1/07: I began in a womb-shaped, den-like cave of branches. I was trying to figure out what animal I was, and then I realized I was a very happy little girl about eight years old. I was alone, but happy and free. I was in a city on a sidewalk. The city was gray and ugly, but I felt alive and happy. I walked up a road that turned into a wide bridge in a very industrial city setting. I stayed on the bridge a while feeling happy, young and free. Then I began to cross the bridge and realized it led into an enormous warehouse. I did not want to go in. I turned around. Behind me was city, ugly and gray but home. I got very, very sad. Then I became annoyed because I could not get off the bridge. I wanted to change visions but that did not work. I wanted to end the meditation but I was still on the bridge. So I let all emotion escape me and entered the warehouse. It was hell, a hellish landscape. I marched through and exited the other side. I was surprised to see the road continue in a beautiful and colorful landscape. I lay down on the grass. I knew it was beautiful, but I could not feel the same excitement. I was older now.

Maria knew that her struggle to quit smoking would be hell, but this ecstatic experience greatly abbreviated her time spent in hell. She has not had a cigarette since that experience. Her naïve eight-year-old self, the part of her who was happy in the gray, polluted city of smoking, was saddened by the hellish warehouse ahead of her, and wanted off the bridge that led to her hell of quitting, but her older self summoned the will to enter the warehouse and pass through to the other side. I knew nothing of what she was working on upon entering this ecstatic trance experience until a week later, thus showing how the postures give direction to the trance experience without the needed direction of a therapist.

Beyond the Unconscious

To this point we have been exploring ways to journey into the unconscious mind to seek the *why* that causes our dysfunctional emotions, behaviors, and thoughts, and to recover from this dysfunction, thus allowing us to become a more functional person. Psychotherapists, including the objectivist cognitive therapist, and insurance companies are generally satisfied with these results and do not seek goals beyond these limited solutions, though some psychologists do look beyond to the personal growth of the client. The potential for further personal growth can bring the person to become more fulfilled and self-actualized among the community of all life on Earth and to become a leader in the journey into the new age. Ecstatic trance provides a way for each person to join this community of leaders.

Ecstatic Trance 75

Learning to become this self-actualized leader as we move into the new age is found in our newly gained ability to journey into the universal mind, a mind not different from our personal mind with its thoughts, feelings, beliefs, and intelligence, whether conscious, subconscious, or unconscious, but one that exists beyond our personal mind. The growing evidence for its existence will be presented in Chapter 8. Though each of us will continue to have our own personal concerns and conflicts, once we have resolved most of our major conflicts and concerns that keep us confined within our personal self-centered mind we will find that ecstatic trance can carry us beyond the world of our unconscious and into the world of the universal mind. This universal mind is seen by a number of writers including Ervin Laszlo and Rupert Sheldrake as an energy field or matrix of information, information of everything that has happened since the beginning of time. This information is available to us through the trance state that suppresses what comes to us through the five senses. This information from the universal mind, like that of the unconscious mind, is generally metaphoric as in the above experience of Maria, answering what is of concern to us at the moment, and is likely not a literal experience of that which has happened at some particular point in the past. Going beyond into the world of the universal mind, the world of the spirits, can bring us new visions of the way life could and should be lived to live sustainably on our one and only Earth and can lead us to find a new sense of creativity and fulfillment in life.

For our ancient hunter-gathering ancestors this world, the universal mind, was the world of the spirits that they so valued, spirits that gave them direction in how to live and to protect and sustain the Earth. The shamans of these hunting and gathering people, both past and present, used and use their rituals of ecstatic trance to heal not just the problems of the individual, but they looked beyond to heal the problems of the family, the community/village and the tribe/nation. The ritual as designed by Felicitas Goodman is very Earth centered as we would expect of the shaman's ritual. After smudging with a herbal smoke for cleansing, Goodman's ritual calls the spirits of each direction, thus setting the stage for following and learning from the spirit guides that come to us in trance. Following these spirit guides of the Earth brings us into a relationship of oneness with the Earth and all life of the Earth. The spirit guides are most often of some animal, but they may be any of the flora, fauna, or substance of the Earth, including the geological features of the Earth. In the era of rationality we have generally considered ourselves superior to all other life on Earth, but when we call upon some animal as our spirit guide, a guide that has something to teach us, this sense of superiority disappears, thus bringing us into a relationship of oneness with that animal and, in turn, with the Earth. This Earth centered mentality is needed as we face such problems as global climate change in our search for ways to save the Earth. This ritual carries us beyond our limited socialized consciousness, the level of consciousness that satisfies the goals of insurance companies, and into the realms of the cultural and spiritual creative (Korten, 2006), realms that can greatly benefit the Earth. These higher levels of consciousness are most important for our species to survive.

Using ecstatic trance to access the universal mind, can bring us in communion with our ancestors as was so important to our hunting-gathering ancestors. My first ancestral experience, an experience that felt to me as if came directly from one of my ancient ancestors, occurred in January of 2010 while using the Hallstatt Warrior Posture (Fig 6.2).

This posture found in Germany is from the 5th century B.C. and has been determined to be a realm of the dead posture:

> I felt myself go back to a much earlier time, probably around 5000 B.C. in Germany, likely one of my places of origin. I was in a thatched hall, long and narrow, that sat near the entrance to a cave. One man, wearing a bearskin, was with me – not the leader but the second or third in command. He told me that the group of men in the hall was preparing to go on a hunt the next morning. Some of the men were drawing in the dirt pictures of animals with spears stuck in them. Others were carving and sharpening the ends of their spears. This one man who stood with me told me that since I was from the future, I must have some wisdom or knowledge that would help in the hunt. I shook my head, "No," but he was insistent that I was to lead them in tomorrow's hunt. We slept on the dirt floor around the fire, and in the morning, though I took the group in what felt to me like a random direction, we did come to several deer. I motioned for the men, about a dozen of them, to spread out, and we herded the deer over a cliff. They all seemed overjoyed in appreciation, though I still felt as if I had done nothing of significance or had no special knowledge.

If this experience were to happen now, it is very unlikely that we would so casually greet someone from the future, though such encounters could have been more common and acceptable during those more magical times with their trust in the spirits. It is true that the descriptions of the hunt and even the practice of herding the deer over a cliff could have come from stories that I have likely heard or read over the years, but, at the time of the experience, the personal message to me was to have more confidence in myself. This ecstatic trance narrative, though, came to me with the awareness that Germany is one of my ancestral homelands and likely with the unspoken intent of visiting my ancestors. This German connection made this trance experience very special. After this experience I have had many ecstatic experiences that have felt as if they came from my own ancestors of Germany and Northern Europe, many of which have been published in the first half of my book, *Baldr's Magic* (2014).

Ecstatic Trance 77

Figure 6.2 Hallstatt Warrior.

Image from *The Power of Ecstatic Trance* by Nicholas E. Brink, PhD published by Inner Traditions International and Bear & Company, ©2013. All rights reserved. www.Innertraditions.com Reprinted with permission of publisher.

Many other similar experiences from the distant past have not necessarily felt ancestral but felt as if they were of the spirits of the land where the experience took place. Some of these spirits of the land are experiences I have written about in *Beowulf's Ecstatic Trance Magic* (2016a). The experiences of the young princess Wealhtheow, the daughter of the chieftain Olaf, who eventually married King Hrothgar from the ancient poem of

Beowulf, revealed to me the struggle that the women of the time felt in their relationship with men who as retainers to the king sought power and fame through the strength of the muscles and ability to fight. One of my ecstatic experiences from *Beowulf's Ecstatic Trance Magic* was of Forsetason, a student of Vanadisdottir, a priestess, healer, and the governess of Queen Wealhtheow. If you recall, Grendel was the monster that terrorized King Hrothgar. Grendel felt threatened by the warrior ways of the king and his retainers, but from my ecstatic experiences I learned that he was at peace with the women of the kingdom in their gentle and compassionate ways. In this experience, again using the Hallstatt Warrior Posture (Fig 6.2), which has become one of the most powerful postures for me, I join Forsetason in his trance experience:

> Later that night Forsetason, when he is awakened in his lean-to on the hillside where he spends his time tending the king's sheep, he hears someone or something coming toward him. It was Grendel. The creature was quiet and did not appear at all agitated as Vanadisdottir had described him in their earlier meeting. Forsetason motions for Grendel to sit down near him, and he does. Grendel begins to move his hands and arms in his own way to communicate, but Forsetason puts up his hand to stop him, pointing to his own head, and then sweeps his hands down over his body to his place of harmony just below his belly button. Then he points to Grendel's head and sweeps his hand down in front of Grendel, pointing to the creature's place of harmony. After doing this several times he can tell that Grendel begins to hear his thoughts and Forsetason knows what Grendel is thinking. He knows that other animals can read one another's minds in this way and that he himself is able to read the minds of animals, especially his sheep. Grendel is thinking that he can trust the shepherd because he was a person of peace who cares for his sheep, and now he discovers that the shepherd even knows what his sheep are thinking. Forsetason nods yes and tells Grendel through his thoughts that he knows that Grendel is hungry and on his way to get a sheep from the king's pen, and Forsetason thinks that is okay. Grendel says that he wants to take it back to the cave to share with his mother, to feed her too, and that tonight he was not going into the great hall where the men are crazy, and that their craziness makes him very angry.

Much is to be learned from the time of transition of those who lived harmoniously with the Earth in the matriarchal era of the hunter-gatherers and those who lived in the patriarchal era of warriors and chieftains. We have much to learn from visiting our ancestors if we of the 21st century are to learn how to live in peace and harmony in the new era that is before us. The spirits of those earlier eras are available to us as we allow ourselves to rediscover the way of the ancients to commune with the spirits by journeying into the universal mind using the power of ecstatic trance.

Spirits of the Earth

Some of us may find it difficult to talk of and find power in the spirits as did our ancient ancestors, and they likely consider these beliefs as no more than superstitious in the present era of rationality, but again, as we will see in Chapter 8, there is considerable research and scientific evidence to validate this world of the spirits, the world of the universal mind. In the coming new age, the era of time-free transparency in using the words of Jean Gebser (1985), we will regain our ability to commune with a consciousness that is beyond the confines of the conscious and unconscious mind that resides within our physical body.

Within the confines of our unconscious mind we have experienced the characters that arise within our nighttime dreams. Considering these dream characters as spirits can be an easy first step for those who might consider the spirits as only superstitious. Similarly, Carl Jung (Campbell, 1971) considered the characters of mythology as characters that come to us from the collective unconscious, and again these archetypal characters can be referred to as spirits when we consider the collective unconscious as beyond the confines of the conscious/unconscious mind that resides within our physical body. Opening ourselves to these spirits, to learning from these spirits as we learn about ourselves from our nighttime dreams and the archetypal nature of our beloved myths, we have much to relearn from that which we have relegated to the domain of superstitions that was of so much value to our ancient ancestors. During the era of rationality we have limited ourselves only to seeing the world through our five senses, but now the sixth sense, the sense of intuition, is again coming alive to us, and it is through the state of trance that it comes alive.

To our ancient ancestors the spirits of all life, the spirits of all flora and fauna, were alive to them as well as the spirits of the flow of water and air, of paths, mountains, valleys, of the soil that supports life, and of stones, all had something to teach them. Those of us who now open ourselves to these spirits are finding value and beauty coming from them. One of my experiences while using the Bahia Metamorphosis Posture (Fig 6.3) revealed to me my struggle of not wanting to go with the flow of the river but then with curiosity I let go of my struggle to explore and find beauty in the pool of water:

> With my tongue hanging out in this posture I feel myself drooling. My tongue is a waterfall coming out of my mouth. I am inside of my mouth, straddling the river flowing out of the cave, which is my mouth. I can't stay straddled over the river, and so eventually I give up and go over the waterfall. On the way down I grab a hanging vine and swing over to the

Figure 6.3 Bahia Metamorphosis.

Image from *The Power of Ecstatic Trance* by Nicholas E. Brink, PhD published by Inner Traditions International and Bear & Company, ©2013. All rights reserved. www.Innertraditions.com Reprinted with permission of publisher.

crotch of a tree in the jungle. I look back at the cave with the tongue hanging out, smooth with a crease in the center. I become curious about what's inside the cave so I swing back to it such that I fly far into it, the cave. The water is coming up from below, shooting up and out the mouth. I slide down the up-flowing water into a pool of water at the bottom, a quiet pool that is open to the outside behind the bottom of the waterfall. I swim out into the beautiful pool from behind the waterfall and climb up on a rock using my left knee. I lay there feeling young, relishing the rainbows I see in the mist of the waterfall.

Watching young children relating to the Earth around them, and recalling the many experiences we had as children in relating to the Earth, of watching a leaf float down a stream, of climbing trees, of looking for four-leaf clovers, shows us the beauty of relating to these spirits of the Earth, but because of the expectations of our parents, because of the importance of what is taught in our schools and religious institutions, this openness to nature that we experienced as children has been lost. But now it can be regained. This is the vision of my book, *Trance Journeys of the Hunter-Gatherers: Ecstatic Practices to Reconnect with the Great Mother and Heal the Earth* (2016b). The experience of David while using the Jama-Coaque Diviner Posture (Fig 6.4) is a good example of recovering the sense of childhood:

I go back in time to when I was young, growing up in cornfields and forests of Illinois. I am getting dirty digging holes, fishing, and lying in the fields, watching the clouds passing in the sky. I run through the forest and see animals, some imaginary ones, coming up from the ground itself and then disappearing. Then I find myself in the fields, creeks, ravines, trails, clearings, bluff lines and sandstone outcrops, shelter bluffs, and forests of Southern Illinois that I know so well. I know all the nuanced shapes and features at various places. Then I move on to Southern Ontario, the lake region, and finally to Western Australia and the area of land on the coast near the small town of Denmark, along the wild Southern Ocean, with its trails, brush, coastal scrub, sand dunes, and seacoast. I see myself as a child especially when I am in Illinois, and later, in Australia, as only a spirit with no body a very pleasant experience.

In the process of psychotherapy we have been satisfied with resolving the presenting problem that brought us to the therapy session, at least the insurance companies are satisfied with this goal and actually are not interested in and do not want to pay for the client to find greater self-actualization in going beyond the immediate goal of problem resolution. But with the current state of world affairs, with the wars, violence, and hate that we are experiencing, to save the Earth and some form of civilization as we know it, we must open ourselves to moving into the new age, and opening the goal of psychotherapy to growth and self-actualization becomes most urgent.

Felicitas Goodman's Earth oriented ritual for inducing ecstatic trance (1990) has been quite effective in giving us direction in finding ways of living sustainably on Earth, but that does not mean that hypnosis can't lead

Figure 6.4 Jama-Coaque Diviner.
Image from *The Power of Ecstatic Trance* by Nicholas E. Brink, PhD. published by Inner Traditions International and Bear & Company, ©2013. All rights reserved. www.Innertraditions.com Reprinted with permission of publisher.

us there too, with the goal of growth and self-actualization. Such hypnotic suggestions as "Open yourself to your untapped potentials for creativity and contribution to the world around you," or "Let the dreams and desires that you have held within you come alive and flourish as you move into your new world of creativity." Ecstatic trance has shown me that this new age will be one of a sense of oneness with the Earth, a sense of community with each other, a sense of harmony and peace, a sense of curiosity and continued learning, and a sense of creativity.

In the next chapter we will examine a specific sequence of ecstatic postures that, like analytic hypnotherapy, follow the steps of cognitive-behavioral therapy, an ecstatic posture sequence that is referred to as *soul retrieval*, i.e. the retrieval of an earlier innocent part of the self that was lost to some early trauma in life that was likely forgotten or repressed. Rather than defining these steps with specific hypnotic suggestions, the steps are defined non-verbally by the postures used in the sequence, postures that accomplish the same thing in the process of therapy as do the hypnotic suggestions of analytic hypnotherapy by first seeking the *why* of the presenting problem.

References

Brink, N. (2013). *The Power of Ecstatic Trance: Practices for Healing, Spiritual Growth, and Accessing the Universal Mind*. Rochester, VT: Bear & Co.

Brink, N. E. (2014). *Baldr's Magic: The Power of Norse Shamanism and Ecstatic Trance*. Rochester, VT: Bear & Co.

Brink, N. E. (2016a). *Beowulf's Ecstatic Trance Magic: Accessing the Archaic Powers of the Universal Mind*. Rochester, VT: Bear & Co.

Brink, N. E. (2016b). *Trance Journeys of the Hunter-Gatherers: Ecstatic Practices to Reconnect with the Great Mother and Heal the Earth*. Rochester, VT: Bear & Co.

Brink, N. E. (2017). *Ecstatic Soul Retrieval: Shamanism and Psychotherapy*. Rochester, VT: Bear & Co.

Campbell, J. (Ed.) (1971). *The Portable Jung*. New York, NY: Viking Press.

Emerson, V. F. (1972). Can Belief Systems Influence Behavior? Some Implications of Research on Meditation. *Newsletter Review*, R. M. Bucke Memorial Society, 5, 20–32.

Gebser, J. (1985). *The Ever-Present Origin*. Athens, OH: Ohio University Press.

Goodman, F. (1990). *Where the Spirits Ride the Wind: Trance Journeys and Other Ecstatic Experiences*. Bloomington, IN: Indiana University Press.

Korten, D. (2006). *The Great Turning: From Empire to Earth Community*. San Francisco, CA: Berrett-Koehler Publishing.

Mair, L. P. (1969). *Witchcraft*. New York, NY: McGraw-Hill.

7 Ecstatic Soul Retrieval and Analytic Hypnotherapy

Ecstatic Soul Retrieval

I first experienced Ecstatic Soul Retrieval (ESR) in 2010 at the Cuyamungue Institute in New Mexico with Ki Salmen (2010), a German instructor of ecstatic trance. During this four day program I realized how parallel ESR is to analytic hypnotherapy, but within the customary psychotherapy setting ESR would appear quite foreign and divergent from what clients would expect in a therapy session. I will begin by describing the process of ESR that I learned from Ki before I describe how the ritual of ecstatic trance can be modified to meet the expectations of the client in psychotherapy. I have previously described these modifications to ESR in my book, *Ecstatic Soul Retrieval: Shamanism and Psychotherapy* (2017).

Central to ecstatic trance and ESR are the ecstatic ritual postures. Thus, to begin, the first of the ecstatic postures to be used is the Bear Spirit Posture, a posture that facilitates healing and increases emotional strength so that the participants in the ESR group have the emotional strength needed to help them face the source of their emotional pain. The Bear Spirit Posture (Fig. 7.1) is from a wood carving of a bear hugging a man, the man standing in this posture with his hands on his abdomen, the place I like to refer to as a person's center of harmony. The carving was found among the indigenous Kwakiutl people of the Pacific Northwest Coast and was from the late 1800s.

For each step in the process of ESR the ecstatic trance ritual as presented in the previous chapter is used. First, after describing to the group the process of ESR and the posture, and after answering any questions that may arise, the participants are smudged with the smoke from a bundle of burning herbs and the spirits of each direction are called in order to define the space as sacred. Five minutes of silence are then observed while the participants focus on their breathing in order to help quiet their minds. After this period of silence the participants stand in the Bear Spirit Posture, and stimulation to the nervous system begins with the rapid beat of a drum or the shaking of a rattle at about 210 beats per minute. This stimulation continues for 15 minutes before it comes to an end. The participants then

Ecstatic Soul Retrieval 85

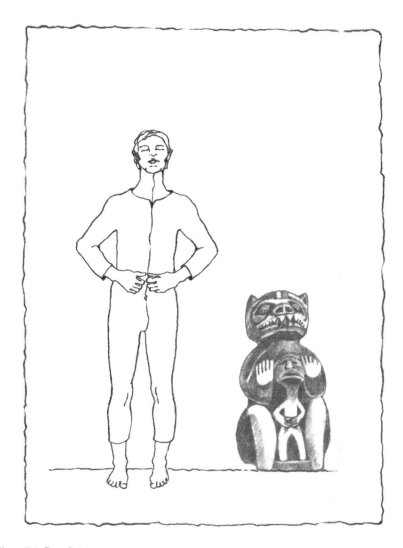

Figure 7.1 Bear Spirit.
Image from *The Power of Ecstatic Trance* by Nicholas E. Brink, PhD published by Inner Traditions International and Bear & Company, ©2013. All rights reserved. www.Innertraditions.com Reprinted with permission of publisher.

slowly come out of trance, record their experiences in their individual journals, and share in turn their ecstatic experience with the rest of the group.

For the second session the participants use a divination posture, asking the diviner for direction or a spirit guide to find resolution to their

86   *Ecstatic Soul Retrieval*

emotional pain or lost souls. I like to use the Lady of Cholula Posture, a pre-Columbian figurine found in Cholula, Mexico from around 1350 A.D. (Fig. 7.2).

The number of possible postures that are used for ecstatic trance has grown substantially since the publication of Felicitas Goodman's book that illustrated approximately 50 postures, but as we go beyond simply collecting and

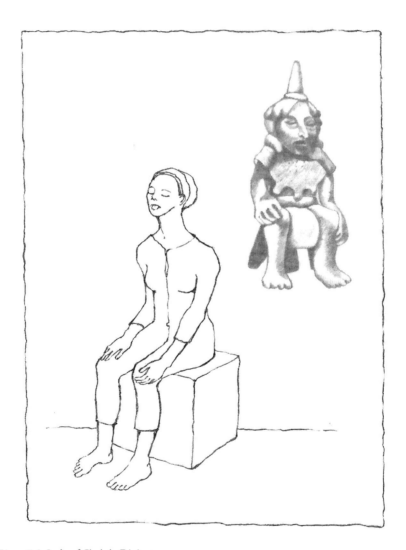

Figure 7.2 Lady of Cholula Diviner.

Image from *The Power of Ecstatic Trance* by Nicholas E. Brink, PhD published by Inner Traditions International and Bear & Company, ©2013. All rights reserved. www.Innertraditions.com Reprinted with permission of publisher.

experimenting with new and different postures, we are beginning to develop protocols for the use of ecstatic trance for different and specific purposes such as ESR. I have found, and so has Ki, that a set of about eight postures is sufficient and most effective in accomplishing the specific goals of the trance experiences. Repeated use and familiarity with a few select postures increases the effectiveness of the intended purpose of these postures. Yet, periodic experimentation with different and occasionally new postures keeps the importance of the postures alive within an individual.

The divination posture is used to ask the diviner for direction. Depending upon the participant's awareness of the presenting problem, a number of different questions might be asked of the diviner, e.g. "Where should I go on this journey?" or "Bring me a spirit guide to lead me on this journey." Though I use the Lady of Cholula Posture because of the natural sense of alertness expressed by the posture in sitting erect while grasping one's knees, Ki's preference is the Olmec Diviner Posture (Fig. 7.3).

Third, we use the Jivaro Under World Posture (Fig. 7.4) of lying on one's back with the back of the wrist of the left hand resting on the forehead for journeying into the under world of the unconscious mind to uncover the source of the presenting problem. In this posture we are also led to uncover the new and healthier language that leads us to resolution of the problem. This posture was found among the Jivaro people of northern Peru and eastern Ecuador at the headwaters of the Marañon River and is described in Michael Harner's book, *Jivaro: People of the Sacred Waterfalls* (1972). Again, lying on one's back is a relatively accepted posture in the context of psychoanalysis, thus it is readily accepted by the client.

Once the new healthier way of thinking becomes evident it is time to use a posture for transformation. The effect of this initiation posture provides a death-rebirth experience with the death of the old dysfunctional way of thinking and the birth of the healthier new way of thinking. I like to use the Feathered Serpent Posture for this purpose (Fig. 7.5), a posture of standing with the backs of your hands resting against your hips and elbows extending outward to either side, a posture that I find expresses a sense of determination, of saying I am ready to make this change in my life. The Feathered Serpent is the goddess of life and fertility, Quetzalcoatl, and she was recognized in this figurine found near Zacatecas, Mexico from between 100 and 650 A.D. It is in the Los Angeles County Museum of Natural History in California.

Another posture I might use is the Olmec Prince Posture (Fig. 7.6) for metamorphosis or shape-shifting. After using the Lady of Cholula Posture for divination, sometimes inserting a session using a shape-shifting posture can bring more alive the beneficial use of the participant's spirit guide. With the knuckles of your hands resting on the ground, a sense of reenacting a four legged animal is apparent, though I have found that this posture easily brings the person to experience a bird, snake, or other creature without four legs.

Figure 7.3 Olmec Diviner.
Image from *The Power of Ecstatic Trance* by Nicholas E. Brink, PhD published by Inner Traditions International and Bear & Company, ©2013. All rights reserved. www.Innertraditions.com Reprinted with permission of publisher.

Sometimes I conclude this sequence of sessions with an upper world posture, a posture that can help celebrate and move these experiences to a more spiritual place. The posture I would use for this purpose is the Venus of Galgenberg (Fig. 7.7) who is reaching to the heavens and gazing upwards in that same direction. This posture is the oldest of the postures we use for ecstatic trance, found in a 32,000-year-old stone figure only 2.75

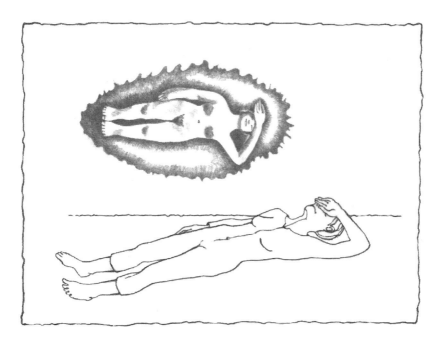

Figure 7.4 Jivaro Under World.
Image from *The Power of Ecstatic Trance* by Nicholas E. Brink, PhD published by Inner Traditions International and Bear & Company, ©2013. All rights reserved. www.Innertraditions.com Reprinted with permission of publisher.

inches tall that was discovered along the bank of the Danube River near Krems, Austria.

In the psychotherapy setting I have not used the above names of these postures. But after the initial use of this set of postures, as the clients begin to be aware of the power of the postures in giving direction to the therapeutic process, they are ready to hear and accept the story of from where these postures came, a story that opens them to a greater sense of diversity in life, of valuing the power used by the ancient shamans of antiquity. In discovering the value of the postures they have begun on their journey of moving beyond their self-centered struggles with their emotional pain and into a world of valuing those of a diverse background different from their own.

Patricia

Upon joining our ecstatic trance group, Patricia mentioned while introducing herself that, though she had always lived in the area, she had just moved back in with her parents and sister who live in a town not far from where our group meets. Soon after she joined the group we decided that over the next

90   *Ecstatic Soul Retrieval*

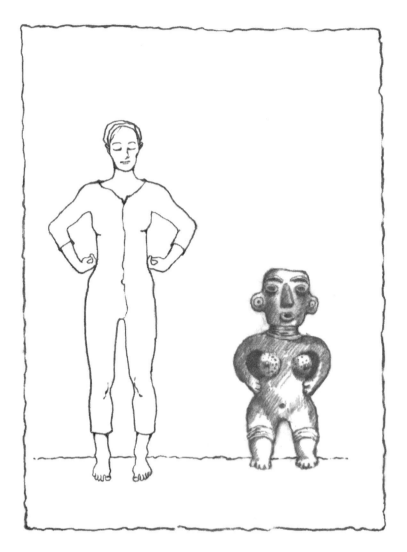

Figure 7.5 Feathered Serpent.

Image from *The Power of Ecstatic Trance* by Nicholas E. Brink, PhD published by Inner Traditions International and Bear & Company, ©2013. All rights reserved. www.Innertraditions.com Reprinted with permission of publisher.

several sessions we would repeat the ESR sequence of postures. The group generally goes through this sequence two or three times a year. After the initial induction ritual of cleansing, calling the spirits, and quieting the mind, we stood in the Bear Spirit Posture (Fig. 7.1) for 15 minutes while I beat the drum.

Ecstatic Soul Retrieval 91

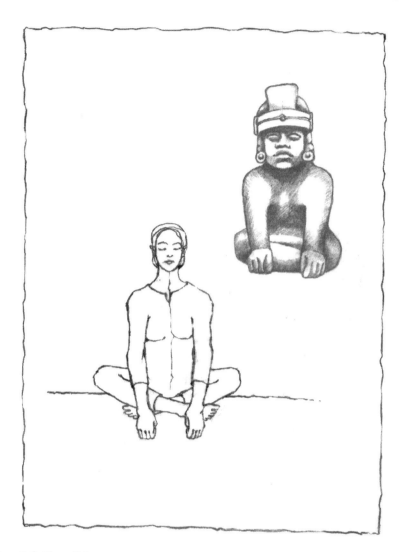

Figure 7.6 Olmec Prince.

Image from *The Power of Ecstatic Trance* by Nicholas E. Brink, PhD published by Inner Traditions International and Bear & Company, ©2013. All rights reserved. www.Innertraditions.com Reprinted with permission of publisher.

This posture is probably the one seen most frequently around the world in most hunting and gathering societies. I have in my collection of trance figures two carved wooden figures standing in this posture from the San Blas Indians of Panama. The people of this society refer to these figures as dream figures. While standing with your hands resting of your abdomen

Figure 7.7 Venus of Galgenberg.

Image from *The Power of Ecstatic Trance* by Nicholas E. Brink, PhD published by Inner Traditions International and Bear & Company, ©2013. All rights reserved. www.Innertraditions.com Reprinted with permission of publisher.

just below your navel, you can feel your abdomen rising and falling with each breath, i.e. if you are breathing correctly from you abdomen, a very natural way of experiencing your breath, thus it is readily accepted as a beneficial posture to use in therapy.

At the end of the 15 minutes Patricia reported that she felt a warm energy flowing into her body with each breath, and as she exhaled this warm healing and strengthening energy spread throughout her body. In presenting and practicing this posture at the very beginning of the ritual I generally comment on the correctness of breathing from the diaphragm rather than from the chest, because the rib cage around the lungs limits their ability to expand and causes a feeling of tightness in your chest. I also mention that when you exhale imagine the inhaled energy spreading throughout your body.

Patricia also described in her experiences a sense of growing taller or standing straighter with each breath, a sense of growing emotional strength.

The following week, after the initial ritual, we used the Lady of Cholula Divination Posture (Fig. 7.2). Though I generally do not specify a specific question to ask the Lady, we do discuss the range of possible questions. At the end of the 15 minutes Patricia reported that she had asked for a spirit guide and what she saw in her experience was a German shepherd dog. Though her family has always had a dog, a small dog, she had always thought of the German shepherd as a very friendly dog like the one her neighbors had. In this experience she was walking down the street in town with the dog on a leash. It was walking at her side and at one point a fairly seedy looking man came walking towards them. She could hear the growl coming from the dog's throat as the man passed them, giving them wide distance. She came to the wall along the edge of the college campus and they sat together on it with Patricia petting her dog. It was a very pleasant experience.

The next week, after our initial ritual, we used the Jivaro Under World Posture (Fig. 7.4), of lying on our backs with the back of the wrist of our left hand resting on our foreheads. In this experience Patricia felt herself slide across the floor and into the under world that turned out to be the darkened living room of her parent's house. She first saw herself looking through the edge of the blinds out a front window. It was daytime but it was darkened inside with the blinds closed and with no lights turned on. She mentioned feeling somewhat frightened or trapped in the house. The house was in a quiet residential neighborhood and what she could see were the bushes and trees in the yards of the houses in the neighborhood. She thought there was nothing to be frightened of, yet she felt this sense of apprehension. Soon her dog came to her with its leash in its mouth. She remembered the German shepherd of one of her friends used to do this when it wanted to go out for a walk. She put the leash on the dog, and they went out and again into town. Again this seedy looking man came walking towards them and the dog growled as it did before. Patricia felt safe and secure when walking with the dog.

Because of Patricia's two experiences with the German shepherd, I decided that we should use the Olmec Prince Posture (Fig. 7.6), for shape-shifting for the next session. At the end of the 15 minutes Patricia reported that she quickly became the German shepherd walking alongside of her on a leash. As the dog she felt quite protective of Patricia and loving towards her, especially when she began petting her as they sat on the wall. As the dog she felt very alert in watching everyone that was nearby. She could feel the feelings coming from others who passed by, and soon one of Patricia's neighbors came walking by and sat with them.

> As the dog I was very comfortable in letting this neighbor pet me. I could smell the smell of her dog on her and knew that she was a dog lover too. But soon the seedy looking man came walking by and I did not trust him. I started to growl. As Patricia I appreciated how the dog was able to distinguish between those who she could trust and who she did not trust.

In considering the logic of the unconscious mind, Patricia taking on the feelings of the German shepherd is an example of displacement.

Following Patricia's report, someone else in the group brought up how it is important to be observant of others and develop this sense of discrimination. At this point Patricia opened up to tell more of her story, that she had been sexually molested by a man when she was walking in a fairly seedy neighborhood with no one else around, a neighborhood near where she used to live before moving back in with her parents, and that she now knew better about where it was safe to walk.

The next week we used the Feathered Serpent Posture (Fig. 7.5), the ancient fertility goddess of Mexico. In this posture, with the backs of your hands resting at your waist with your elbows extending outward to either side, a feeling of determination is experienced. Patricia was quick to sense this feeling of determination expressed in this posture and recognized it as a determination to pay more attention to the world around her and make the discriminations of when this world was safe and when it was dangerous. She could feel the discriminating energy of her German shepherd within her and felt a renewed sense of self-confidence in her life, self-confidence that was lost when she had been sexually molested. She could now say that she no longer felt like a victim and realized that the seedy man walking towards her was more the victim in his world.

With these experiences it is important to recognize the several advantages in using the ecstatic trance ritual with the ecstatic postures. One is that the participant needs not to reveal to the group the nature of the problem being faced. Using analytic hypnotherapy the client is expected to reveal the nature of the presenting problem and the therapist provides strategies in how to overcome the problem, e.g. leading the client to determine what was or is needed from an abuser. Then in analytic hypnotherapy the client is led to become the healthier person by living and understanding these needs when relating the needs of others. With ecstatic trance, the postures themselves provide this direction.

Also, with analytic hypnotherapy, direction is offered in the form of words, and the client is cognitively involved. With ecstatic trance a somatic dimension is added thus the participant is more totally involved in the process, and generally many less words are used. The concluding section of this chapter will offer suggestions as to how the postures can be integrated within analytic hypnotherapy, and how a few hypnotic words along with the postures can provide an even more effective approach to the therapy.

A third factor is the use of rapid drumming instead of quiet new age music that is often used with hypnosis. For the client who tends to be easily distracted by internal dialogue, tends to be more hyper, and is not adept in quieting the mind, the rapid drumming or rattling may be more effective for inducing trance because the rapid stimulation to the nervous system becomes an effective distraction to the internal dialogue.

The trance experiences are also different. The calming parasympathetic nervous system dominates with hypnotic trance. Though in this trance state there are times when emotions are aroused and a sympathetic response occurs, in general the hypnotic state is one of relaxation and rest. On the other hand, the sympathetic nervous system dominates when ecstatic trance is induced with rapid stimulation to the nervous system. The sympathetic response is one of activation. The experience of near death is a common experience with ecstatic trance.

Carlos Castaneda also describes two ways to enter "the realm of the inorganic beings," (1993, p. 187), or in my words, the realm of the spirits or the universal mind. One way is through *dreaming* and the other through *stalking*. Dreaming "is when awareness picks up the sorcerer's energy body and takes it wherever it may" (1993, p. 186). These words suggest a sense of spontaneity, that the sorcerer's energy body is carried without intent but with awareness into the other world, "into the realm of the inorganic beings." What is this energy body? Castaneda continues, "Human beings are composed of an incalculable number of threadlike energy fields ... an encased agglomeration that manifests itself as a ball of light the size of the person's body ... like a giant luminous egg." (1987, p. 15). Similarly, hypnosis is letting go of conscious intent like the spontaneity of nighttime dreaming as one journeys into the other world, the world of the inorganic beings.

On the other hand *stalking* seems quite parallel or equivalent to ecstatic trance, i.e. it "is when the sorcerer decides, in full consciousness, to use the avenue of awareness to make the journey (Castaneda, 1993, p. 187)." The journey is made with intent. "Intent is the pervasive force that causes us to perceive. We do not become aware because we perceive, rather, we perceive as a result of the pressure and intrusion of intent" (Castaneda, 1987, p. 16). Though we begin the journey fully consciousness and with intent, we may exit this conscious awareness as we become distracted by the rapid stimulation to the nervous system, distracted by drumming or other similar activities of stimulation.

Integrating ESR and Analytic Hypnotherapy

In the setting of the psychotherapist's office, the expectations of the client would differ greatly from what Patricia experienced. Smudging and calling the spirits from each direction especially would be seen as quite bizarre. In that quiet new age music is often played in the background in the customary setting of psychotherapy, playing a recording of drumming or rattling can be explained sufficiently such that the client is not unnerved by it. I like to explain that many people who are bothered by a racing mind and who have a difficult time focusing or quieting their mind in order to relax find that drumming can be a distraction for their busy mind, and find that it can help them relax. Similarly, the initial four ecstatic postures that I use in a therapy session, with sufficient explanation, can fit adequately within a person's expectations, e.g. lying on your back on the therapist's couch with the wrist of your left hand resting on your forehead is an acceptable posture for the psychoanalyst and is thus easily accepted by the client. As we will see in the next case study, when the client sits or stands in the other three postures, and the feelings that each posture causes the client to experience are examined and discussed, the purpose of the posture makes sense and is thus easily accepted by the client. Thus, these elements of ecstatic trance are easily incorporated in the therapy session.

As the process of therapy continues I like to refer to the characters and objects within a dream or hypnotic experience as spirits or spirit guides that have something to teach and are valued. It generally does not take long for the client to become comfortable in talking about the spirits and spirit guides. After the client has experienced the initial four postures, I will likely tell the story about the meaning and use of these postures, from where these postures came, and of the importance of the spirits and spirit guides in shamanic healing. The eventual consequence in explaining the meaning of calling the spirits can be the use of the litany for calling the spirits. The litany is a way of defining the space being used as special or sacred, and though the therapy room easily becomes a special place, a place of confidentiality and openness, the litany of calling the spirits adds to focusing on the spirits and increases the diversity in the way the client experiences the world. This increased focus on the spirits is a step away from the self-centeredness experienced in the client's struggle with the personal problems that brought them to therapy, and a step towards becoming a cultural creative in valuing a broader diversity of people.

Parallels between Analytic Hypnotherapy and the Ecstatic Postures

Analytic hypnotherapy generally begins with a hypnotic exercise to teach relaxation and increase emotional strength. As the client is led into trance, in addition to the words to invoke the *yes-set*, such words as "Every day in every way feel your strength and self-confidence growing within you," intensifies the feel of relaxation and emotional strength. Also, the experience is intensified by using the Bear Spirit Posture (Fig. 7.1).

> With your hands on your abdomen, feel with each breath the increased sense of relaxation and emotional strength as your abdomen rises, and as you exhale and your abdomen falls let these feels of relaxation and emotional strength flow and spread throughout your body.

Thus, adding the Bear Spirit Posture to the initial hypnotic exercise for relaxation and increased emotional strength makes considerable sense. The words of relaxation and growing emotional strength are used initially with each breath so that with practice the hypnotic repetition of these words becomes less important and their use is diminished.

With each of the following steps in the process of analytic hypnotherapy, the Bear Spirit Posture is used to induce trance with its relaxation and increased emotional strength. The next steps are to lead the client in identifying the feelings associated with the presenting problem and to carry these feelings back through time to their source using the *affect bridge* and *age regression*. For the client to clarify these feelings, the divination posture can be used, asking the diviner for help in identifying and clarifying these feelings. To do this I would use the Lady of Cholula divination posture of sitting erect and grasping one's knees, a posture that provides a sense of anticipation while waiting for the answer after having asked the Lady for help in identifying and clarifying these feelings.

Having identified these feelings, I would proceed in using the *affect bridge* with its suggestions of carrying the feelings back through time while the client is lying on his or her back on the couch with the wrist of the left hand resting on the forehead in what is the Jivaro Posture. Carrying the feelings or affect of the emotional pain on this journey back through time into the under world of the unconscious mind carries the identified feelings back to their source. At this point, when the source is reached, a beginning hypnotic suggestion in the healing process would be, "Let your adult self be with your younger self, and with all the wisdom and understanding of your adult self, help your younger self understand." The words, "with all the wisdom and understanding of your adult self," add to the client's sense of self-confidence. With the client identifying this early experience that triggered these feelings, I will often suggest that they go further back in time to uncover an even earlier experience.

For the next session while again using the Jivaro Under World Posture I would hypnotically suggest that the client again go back in time to these earlier experiences, and "With all the wisdom and understanding of your adult self, let your adult self help your younger self in finding the right words to describe what is needed that would have prevented these early experiences from happening." In stating these words of what is needed the client is led to state these needs in the positive and in as many different ways as possible, e.g. "Dad, I need you to be gentle and patient," and "Mom, I need you to listen carefully to what I have to say."

The following session would then be the time to use the Feathered Serpent initiation or death-rebirth posture with the hypnotic suggestion to become the words or integrate within yourself the words of what you needed to prevent the early experiences from happening, e.g. "Let your adult self become these words, let your adult self become gentle and understanding," or "Let your adult self become the good listener when listening to others."

Finally, while again using the Feathered Serpent Posture the hypnotic suggestion is that the client practice using these words of what is needed in relating to others, e.g. "Be gentle and understanding in your relationships with others," or "Be the protector in helping others." While in trance and using the Feathered Serpent Posture the client rehearses being this healthier person at home and also in his or her regular activities of living in relating to others. This final step is an effective way to reinforce the *cognitive-emotional experience*, and these experiences are reinforced as they are described in the next several therapy sessions.

Both the under world posture and the Feathered Serpent Posture are each likely repeated over more than one session. First, for journeying into the unconscious to find a solution to the problem the Jivaro Under World Posture is used, and then the Feathered Serpent is used for the practice of integrating within what has been learned, though the names of these postures are not used initially. Also, there are frequently several dimensions or layers to the presenting problem such that this entire procedure may be repeated several times through the course of psychotherapy.

In considering the integration of shamanic ecstatic trance with psychotherapy, initially clients are quite self-centered in their focus on the emotional pain of the presenting problems they bring to therapy, but as therapy progresses and these clients begin to use what is learned in forming healthy relationships with others their self-centeredness is diminished and their world begins to broaden to include the family, friends, and co-workers, people who are more or less of like minds. With the introduction of some of these shamanic ecstatic trance concepts, this world again broadens to include greater cultural diversity, and greater openness to the world around them, another advantage of offering an explanation of the ecstatic postures. Though this broadening of the client's world is generally of no interest to the insurance companies that may be paying for the therapy sessions, this personal growth is important to the community as a whole.

Chuck

To offer an example of analytic hypnotherapy using the ecstatic postures, Chuck came to therapy because of a problem with periodic panic attacks. During the first session he happened to mention that his last panic attack happened soon after his boss at work mentioned that his sales were down about 2% from the month before, but he didn't think that comment should have caused a panic attack. With some questioning he added that he had been on this job for about two years, and for each month of work his sales had always gone up.

Usually during the first session, after listening to the client's story, if there is time, I offer the relaxation and emotional strengthening exercise using the Bear Spirit Posture, though I did not use that name to describe the posture. This exercise is especially helpful for a person suffering with anxiety or panic attacks, and it needs to be learned during a time when anxiety or panic is not being experienced when the greatest effect of relaxation can be felt. It is difficult to relax during a time of experiencing anxiety. I had Chuck stand and place his hands on his abdomen and instructed him to breathe such that he could feel his abdomen rise and fall with each breath. This took a couple of minutes but soon I could see his breathing move down to his abdomen. I explained to him that breathing from his chest was restricted by his ribs and often caused him to feel tightness in his chest, which we quickly saw was part of the problem for him.

I then turned on a CD of five minutes of rapid drumming that played quietly in the background, explaining to him that the drumming was to distract his overactive mind, allowing him to focus on his breathing. He began to relax while we both stood with our hands on our abdomens. I occasionally offered a few words of suggestion, repeating them several times throughout the five minutes, "With each breath feel the strengthening flow of relaxing energy enter your abdomen and as you exhale let the strengthening and relaxing energy flow throughout your body." While we both stood in the posture for about five minutes, I could see his breathing rate slow, and I could feel him relax.

He reported that with this exercise he felt a sense of strength flow within him. As he left I gave him a copy of the drumming CD and suggested that he practice this exercise for about five minutes each day before the next session.

During the second session, since Chuck was already quite aware of the feeling of panic, the plan was to use the affect bridge to carry the feeling back through time to its source. I had him sit on the edge of his chair with his back straight and grasping his knees in the Lady of Cholula Posture, though I again did not use this name for the posture. I asked him what sitting in this way felt like. With a little discussion he soon became aware of the feeling of alert anticipation as if waiting in anticipation for something. I suggested that what he was waiting for was an answer to the question of what was the source of his panics of when they first began.

Chuck and I then stood with our hands on our abdomen for about five minutes to help him relax and feel a sense of strength flow through his body as the drumming played quietly in the background. We then both sat at the edge of our seats grasping our knees while the drumming continued for the 15 minutes. Though the breathing exercise is trance inducing, in order to deepen the trance, I add the *yes-set* suggestions,

> with your hands grasping your knees, feel the hardness of your knees and the roughness of the material of your jeans with your fingers. Feel your feet planted on the floor and the straightness of your spine, feel the sense of anticipation of sitting in this way.

Soon I moved on to the words of the *affect bridge*,

> Let yourself begin to go back in time, carrying with you your feelings of anxiety and panic. Watch the days go by as you go back in time, the months go by, the years go by as you go back in time carrying your feeling of anxiety and panic with you.

I continued repeating these words or variations on these words, speaking the words slowly at the rate of Chuck breathing. After a few minutes I added the words,

> As you go back in time, you will soon come to a time early in your life when you first started having panic attacks. Let the years go by, and when you reach that time, lift the index finger of your left hand (or whatever finger is the most visible to me) to let me know that you are there.

I repeated these words a few times, lengthening the periods of silence between them. I could see and feel that he was in a good trance. After a while Chuck lifted his finger.

I suggested, "Keep your eyes closed and be where you are. As you stay where you are, tell me what you are experiencing. First, where are you?"

Chuck answered that he was in school, in high school, and he just got back a chemistry test and his score was only a "B." He had always gotten "As," and generally a score of 100%.

I then suggested, "Let your adult self go back and be with your high school self and with all the wisdom and understanding of your adult self, help your high school self understand."

Chuck responded, "I always try so hard, I want to do my best, ... I want to be perfect."

I then suggested, "Go back farther in time, let the time go by, carrying the feelings of panic back to an earlier time. When you are ready, again lift the index finger of your left hand."

It didn't take long before Chuck's finger lifted, and I asked, "What's going on?"

I am at home and my mother asked to see the results of the test I took a couple of days before. I showed her. I think I had gotten 94% and she looked to see what I had missed, and said that I should have know those answers. She expected me to get 100%.

I say, "Okay, again let your adult self go back and be with your younger self, and with all the wisdom and understanding of your adult self, help your younger self understand."

The session was about over, but in our brief discussion I brought up the question, "Was your mother being fair?" and suggested, "She was not letting you be a kid."

In this session, though we were using the Lady of Cholula Posture in seeking an answer to his question, since Chuck was ready to search for the source of his feelings we continued with this posture as he journeyed into his unconscious rather than using the Jivaro Under World Posture. We will use the Jivaro Posture in the next session. Flexibility is using these postures as warranted, and they are still effective.

In the next session we followed the same routine as the session before, but this time I had Chuck lay on the couch with his head to the right end of the couch such that his left arm might have hung off the couch, suggesting that he rest the wrist of that hand on his forehead, the Jivaro Under World Posture. He was quick to recognize that some therapists have their clients lay on a couch all the time. I suggested that the posture does help the client go into their unconscious mind. Then after five minutes of standing with our hands on our abdomen to relax and to increase our emotional strength, I had him lay on the couch in this way, as I laid back in my recliner with my left wrist too on my forehead.

As the drumming played, I suggested, "Go back to when you showed your test paper to your mother." After a few minutes of silence, I asked him, "What is going on?"

Chuck reported that his mother had just told him that he could have done better, and that he was feeling panicked.

So I picked up with, "Let your adult self go back and be with your younger self and help your younger self think of what you needed to hear from your mother instead of 'you could have done better.'"

Chuck began with my suggestion of the last session, "I need my mom to let me be a kid." It was apparent that he had thought about this over the week.

"Okay, say that to your mother, the spirit mother inside of you."

"Mom, I am only ten years old, I sometimes make mistakes."

"Good. Now think of other things you would like to tell her about what a ten year old needs."

After a few minutes, he added,

> Mom, I need time to be with my friends and to play. I am only ten years old. I am doing very well in school, better than all the other kids. Some of them give me a hard time about being too good. I need to relax and enjoy the other kids at school.

"Did she listen to your stories of your play with the other children?"

"I don't remember that she did. I felt different from the other kids and I don't remember having any close friends."

With further discussion in this direction, I suggested,

> As you leave spend some time this week thinking about the mother inside of you, your spirit mother, of how you would have liked your mother to relate to you, of what you would have liked to hear her say, and how you could relate to others in that way.

In the next session we again followed the same procedure, but I showed Chuck a new posture. I had him stand with the backs of his hands at his waist with his elbows extending out in either direction. In talking about the feelings generated by this posture, the Feathered Serpent Posture, he soon came to the feeling of determination expressed by the posture. I suggested that in standing in this posture while listening to the drumming, he could feel the determination of letting his need to be perfect die, and that he could feel a new feeling of being the good listening mother for others in his life.

This time, after the relaxation exercise using the Bear Spirit Posture, we stood with the backs of our hands at our waist as I started the drumming. After the 15 minutes Chuck reported that he felt a new commitment, the commitment of listening to the stories of others. I commented that really listening to others will bring others closer to you and make you a better salesman.

With the insights that these postures provided him he now could see their value and was ready to hear the story of their shamanic origin, thus taking him into a world of greater diversity.

We continued for several more sessions while I listened to his stories of his new effectiveness in listening to others without the challenging comments like those that were made by his boss, teacher, and mother. He reported on new feelings of closeness in his relationships with others and his panic attacks ended. We used the Feathered Serpent Posture several more times to reinforce this new behavior by bringing alive these new experiences while in trance. During these last several sessions, since we had been referring to his trance images as spirits and spirit guides, I also introduced him to the litany of calling the spirits which added to the importance of listening to the spirits and increased the breadth of the diversity of experiences in his life. At the end of therapy I invited him to join the ecstatic trance group where he could meet a number of people who valued the experiences of ecstatic trance and would additionally broaden his world of diversity in moving towards becoming a cultural creative.

This procedure resolved, at least for the time being, his panic attacks, but from past experience there are likely "more layers to the onion," more issues with which to deal such that in the course of psychotherapy this procedure of analytic hypnotherapy using the postures of ecstatic trance will likely be repeated to overcome the deeper issues that are likely to arise. My two books, *Ecstatic Soul Retrieval* (2017) and *Grendel and His Mother* (2002), offer a number of full length case studies that show how this procedure is repeated with variations on the procedure used besides hypnosis and ecstatic trance, dream work and guided imagery, all of which can be effective in producing deeper resolution to personal problems.

References

Brink, N. E. (2002). *Grendel and His Mother: Healing the Traumas of Childhood through Dreams, Imagery and Hypnosis*. Amityville, NY: Baywood Publishing.

Brink, N. (2013). *The Power of Ecstatic Trance: Practices for Healing, Spiritual Growth, and Accessing the Universal Mind*. Rochester, VT: Bear & Co.

Brink, N. E. (2017). *Ecstatic Soul Retrieval: Shamanism and Psychotherapy*. Rochester, VT: Bear & Co.

Castaneda, C. (1987). *The Power of Silence: Further Lessons of Don Juan*. New York, NY: Simon & Schuster.

Castaneda, C. (1993). *The Art of Dreaming*. New York, NY: HarperCollins.

Harner, M. J. (1972). *Jivaro: People of the Sacred Waterfalls*. New York: NY: Doubleday/Natural History Press.

Salmen, A. K. (2010). *Mohnfrau: Wege zur Heilung durch Trance*. Uhlstädt-Kirchhasel, Germany: Arun-Verlag.

8 Evidence for the Universal Mind

In spite of some lingering prejudices against believing in the universal mind, of a world of spirits beyond the self, there is growing undeniable evidence for the universal mind, i.e. a mind beyond the mind that we experience personally as our own. Also, regarding prejudices that come from religious beliefs, there are those who deny the usefulness of hypnosis. On a couple of occasions when speaking of hypnosis I have been confronted with an opposing belief that the use of hypnosis is of the devil. Similarly, in speaking in a college classroom of the spirits that arise in shamanic use of ecstatic trance, one student interrupted, "I believe in only one spirit, the Holy Spirit." When we consider that the elements of our nighttime dreams are from beyond our five senses and thus can be considered "spirits," a new world opens to us. The ways of the shamans are gradually making some inroads into the practice of psychotherapy as is evident in the popularity of presentations on shamanism at the conferences of the International Association of the Study of Dreams. I believe these prejudices are gradually dissolving.

Beyond these prejudices some of the evidence for this "new world," yet an old world to our hunting-gathering ancestors, comes from the field of quantum physics, evidence that even Albert Einstein called spooky (Wolchover, 2017). In this chapter we will review this evidence beginning with Rupert Sheldrake's morphic field (1995), and then Ervin Laszlo's description of the Akashic field (2007), fields that contain all information of everything that has happened since the beginning of time, information that is in-formation within a holographic matrix. Next the spooky research of quantum physics on non-local coherence and quantum entanglement will be presented. We will then move on to the meta-analysis research of Dean Radin (2006) and Gregg Braden (2007) that demonstrates the reality of extrasensory perception, perception that is from beyond our five senses of sight, sound, taste, smell, and touch, and perceives that which is beyond ourselves, from a sixth sense that we sometimes call intuition.

Rupert Sheldrake

Rupert Sheldrake (1995), former director of studies in biochemistry and cell biology at Cambridge University, begins his thesis with the premise that since the universe is held together by gravitational fields and the atom and subatomic particles by electromagnetic fields, and since the cells of our body are composed of atoms, our cells must also exist within such an energy field, a field he calls a morphic field. Carrying this concept further, the organs of the body are composed of cells so that each organ has its own morphic field, fields that communicate with each other to keep the organs of the body in a healthy biochemical balance. Each human exists within its morphic field, and all humans as a species exist within the broader human morphic field. Each species of life similarly exists within the species' morphic field that determines much of what happens in life including the direction of evolution.

Sheldrake gives numerous examples of the effect of the morphic field or of how the field gives direction. When watching a large flock of birds swooping and turning in unison and recognizing that no one bird is in the lead or the leader, it is Sheldrake's belief that their morphic field is what holds them together and gives each bird the information as when to swoop or turn. Another example that occurred a number of years ago is that of the blue tit, a small bird that first learned to go to the doorstep of homes in England where bottles of milk were delivered and peck off the cap of the bottle to take a drink of milk. It wasn't long before this new habit of the blue tit spread throughout England and over the channel to the tits throughout Europe. It was through the tit's morphic field and the process of morphic resonance that this new way of behaving spread, a habit that was inherited collectively.

The process of morphic resonance within the morphic field determines the direction of evolution for all living creatures and also non-living substances. For example, when a newly synthesized chemical compound is created for the first time, as the same compound is crystallized again and again, the crystals tend to form more readily worldwide just because they have already formed somewhere else. Such inheritance of a habit is not just a matter of chemical genes, but an inherited habit that depends upon the transmission of the habit from the previous countless expressions of the habit that occurred in the past. With each expression of the habit, the habit occurs more quickly and easily, a process that I earlier referred to as *kindling* or in using Sheldrake's words, *morphic resonance*.

Considering the evolutionary process of what happens in nature as the evolution of habits rather than preexisting historic and definable laws of nature is Sheldrake's hypothesis of *formative causation*. Historically and until recently, science has searched for *the laws of nature* as eternal laws that have always existed since and even before the beginning of time rather than habits that develop within nature. Science has considered all life on Earth as the product of evolution, a random process, whereas the universe of classical physics is mechanical, with the movement of cosmic bodies determined by the laws of mechanics, sort of like the movements of a clock. But the more recent cosmologists recognize that the universe too has evolved with nuclear reactions that have occurred in the formations of stars that have produced many of the chemical elements that we rely upon today, an evolution that can better be described through *formative causation* with the elements being created through new evolutionary habits. The cosmos too is thus alive and constantly evolving with this evolution occurring within the morphic field of each element, substance, and creature of the cosmos and of our living Earth, Gaia.

In the 1920s several biologists proposed the concept of a morphogenetic field as a mechanism that gave direction in both the process of differentiation of cells and tissues in the embryonic development of organ systems and guided the process of regeneration after damage, but the nature of these fields and how they worked was not clearly understood. Sheldrake has expanded on this subject, attempting to describe the nature of these fields and how they work with the hypothesis of *formative causation*, which influences the fields of subsequent similar systems, and this influence can occur at a distance in both space and time without the influence declining because of this distance. From quantum physics this influence at a distance is the concept of *non-local coherence*.

Sheldrake's recognition that the influence of the morphic field does not diminish and is free of space and time portends the *time-free and transparent* nature of consciousness for the new age as described by Jean Gebser, as we will explore in more depth in the next chapter. The title of Gebser's book, *The Ever Present Origin* (1984), suggests that our origin in the hunter-gatherer culture with their ability to commune with the spirits, is again becoming available to us as we learn to access the information provided by the morphic field, or in other words the spirit world or the universal mind, while in an altered state of trance. This *Ever Present Origin* is also seen in embryonic development. The earliest stages of many embryos all look the same independent of the species, e.g. they all have the gill slits of our ancient fish ancestors. But, as the embryo develops, the features of the species it is to become begin to become more evident, i.e. the cells and tissues begin to differentiate through the process of *formative causation* and *morphic resonance*.

With regard to memory, Sheldrake suggests that the nerve cells of the brain determine how memories are stored, but storage itself is within the morphic fields of the nerve cells. This would allow for generalization, e.g. chairs come in so many different shapes and styles, but somehow we know that each is a chair and that the morphic field for a chair allows for us to generalize to say it is a chair.

These fields go beyond the individual such that there is a field that includes all humans, and similarly fields that contain other species of life. These fields beyond the individual contain information or memory of all that has happened since the beginning of time. It is this broadest morphic field that I call the *Universal Mind*, and it is from this universal morphic field that we draw information that we experience as extrasensory perception. Accessing this field that is beyond the individual's morphic field is something that was commonly experienced by our hunter-gatherer ancestors, information that they considered coming from the spirit world. We have lost this ability to access the spirit world because during this last 2500 years of the era of rational consciousness we have limited our perceived world to the five senses, the senses of sight, sound, taste, smell, and touch. Only as we learn to suppress this limited perception by going into an altered state of consciousness such as hypnotic or ecstatic trance can we again open ourselves to the broader morphic field, the world of the spirits, and thus regain the intuition that was so important to our ancestors.

Ervin Laszlo

Ervin Laszlo's Akashic field (2007, 2009) is similar to if not the same as Sheldrake's morphic field. The word Akashic is a Sanskrit word meaning cosmic sky or space and "refers not only to space in a modern sense but also, and above all, to the higher spheres of life and existence" (Laszlo, 2009, p. 3).

> An Akashic experience is a real, lived experience that conveys a thought, an image, or an intuition that was not, and very likely could not have been transmitted by our five senses either at the time it happened or at anytime beforehand, at least not in our current lifetime.
> (2009, p. 1)

Mainstream science considers the brain the site of memory with input from the five senses, but these Akashic experiences are of revelations that come from sources other than the five senses, sources that are *non-local* or that come from the *non-local mind*. He describes some amazing research that shows that "When the brain of one individual is stimulated in some way the brain of a distant and paired individual, whether a twin, spouse, sibling, or parent-child, demonstrates the same change" as seen in electroencephalograms and functional magnetic resonance imaging. A British author, David Lorimer, calls these connected experiences *empathetic resonance* (Laszlo, 2009, p. 233). These experiments demonstrate that communication or connection between two individuals can occur without going through our five senses and thus is non-local. Laszlo's work takes us beyond the work of Sheldrake by describing how these fields, whether morphic or Akashic, work for the storage of information.

To describe how these fields work for the storage of information Laszlo draws upon the work of Walter Schempp (Laszlo, 2009, pp. 248–249) who suggests that just as the intersection of laser beams of light can produce a stable coherent hologram, so can the expanding waves of the universe propagated from the time of the Big Bang. The research of Kitaev and Pitkanen (Laszlo, 2009, p. 246) shows that networks of quantum particles organize in specific ways such as "weaving" or "braiding" and appear to be sufficiently robust to maintain quantum coherence. The weavings or braids can be the means of holographically storing information in the matrix of the universal memory.

To access this holographic matrix Hameroff (Laszlo, 2009, p. 250) describes the cytoskeletal structure of the brain as proteins organized in a network of microtubules connected to each other structurally by a protein cellular network of vastly more elements than the neuronal network. The human brain has approximately 10^{11} neurons but the cytoskeletal structure has 10^{18} microtubules. Previously the cytoskeleton "was thought to have a purely structural role, but recent evidence indicates that it also conveys signals and processes information … In the emerging consensus, the network of microtubules, with its quantum-scale lattice structure, is the physiological basis of quantum holography in our brain." Rather than our brain being just a site of stored information, with this cytoskeletal structure it is also a site of the reception of information from the universal memory field.

Laszlo describes this information that is found in this holographic matrix as being *in-formation* and is available to us as it was for our ancient hunter-gathering ancestors. He recognizes the reality of extrasensory consciousness, of people who are effective in mental telepathy and communicating with the dead, people who have premonitions of coming events, whether natural or man-made, and people who use these skills to promote healing. He talks of these people and those of ancient and primitive cultures, of shaman and others who seem to have perfected or are more open to such extrasensory consciousness as a necessity for their survival.

> So called primitive people have long known of such "transpersonal" links. Medicine men and shamans appear capable of inducing telepathy through solitude, concentration, fasting, chanting, dancing, drumming, or psychedelic herbs. Whole clans seem able to remain in touch with each other no matter where their members roam.
>
> (Laszlo, 2007, p. 150)

Yet, except for a few exceptional people, we seem to have lost this extrasensory ability, though Laszlo believes that we can again cultivate it. The common denominator of the list of ways to induce telepathy is that these ways are in the altered states of consciousness, trance states that suppress overly rational thought.

Evidence of the energy beams or strings of energy that form the holographic matrix of *in-formation* is occasionally experienced in different forms while in an altered state of consciousness. Robert Waggoner (2009), in his book on lucid dreaming, has asked of the dream the question, "What is behind the dream?" or "Where does the dream come from?" Waggoner experienced the answer to these questions when he saw a blue light. As

Waggoner, who is adept at lucid dreaming, explains, "I needed to journey beyond all symbol, appearance, and illusion, beyond all self-creation, beyond the lucid dream. I needed to find the source of it all. Only then would I truly know if meaning existed behind appearance" (p. 79). Beyond the blue light he eventually concluded that "Within the aware light, there was no idea of self, of me or mine. There were no thoughts, memories, or analysis, no Robert – only a light filled knowing" (p. 81).

In my work with ecstatic trance I have collected a number of experiences similar to seeing blue light or energy in a matrix or grid, as strands of fibers. For example, Susanne, while in ecstatic experience reported,

> I see huge strands of DNA, vibrating, undulating, intertwining, and moving very fast. The DNA seems like a huge paper Chinese dragon in a parade. I have a strong feeling the DNA is very driven with purpose, the purpose being that of evolution into higher forms of being. It cannot be stopped. As myself doing the exercise, I am shaking and undulating too. I feel energy intertwining, going up my spine. I dance with the DNA.

John Lamb Lash (2006, pp. 171–172) beautifully describes this string of energy:

> The German word *Geist*, "spirit," comes from the Indo-Iranian root *ghei*, "to move powerfully." These supreme cosmic beings move powerfully, they are not entities but immense, living currents. The currents surge and circulate, merge, divide, subside, and surge again. The gods dance.

The ancients' world of the spirit is the world of the universal mind, the world of these powerfully moving currents.

The ancient testimony of the Gnostic Mysteries

> attests to the sublime encounter with the Divine Light. This form of luminosity does not appear to ordinary awareness, owing to the filters of human perception, including the egoic filter. The mental gloss of self-reflection is like light shining on a window pane that makes it impossible to see through the window. Once the ego melts away, the parameters of perception are shifted and the Light is there, a substantial presence in the world, soft, white, and shadowless. It is also sentient, animated and animating, aware of itself and what comes into contact with it.
>
> (Lash, 2006, p. 217)

Similarly, in the words of Carlos Castaneda, "the universe is an infinite agglomeration of energy fields, resembling threads of light ... These energy fields, called the Eagle's emanations, radiate from a source of inconceivable proportions metaphorically called the Eagle" (1987, p. 15).

Quantum Physics

The string theory of physics, the theory that has most recently been accepted by the mainstream physics community, is a possible bridge to unite all other theories. Basically it says that the universe is composed of tiny vibrating strings of energy that can be used to explain the observations of both the quantum and everyday worlds.

Non-local communication or *non-local coherence* has its roots in the arena of quantum physics. The non-local parallels in quantum physics that demonstrate non-local communication are seen in the quanta, whether matter, force, or light, and are not entirely separate realities because once they have shared the same state they remain interlinked forever without the expenditure of energy no matter how far they may be from each other. One amazing feature is that when one property of a quantum is measured, other properties of the quantum become unavailable to observation and measurement. If energy is measured then measurement of position is unavailable, other quanta linked with the first will take on the same state with the same measurable and unmeasurable properties. If an experimental situation is created to measure one trait, all other linked quanta will take on that characteristic or state even if the experiment is not carried out.

The Power of Extrasensory Perception

Many thousand experiments of psychic or psi phenomena, whether of the possibility of mental telepathy, clairvoyance, remote viewing, influencing the role of dice, and other psi phenomena, have been performed over the last century to demonstrate the validity of such phenomena. These research experiments have provided minimal support for these psychic phenomena. Often the results of these experiments were in the right direction to validate the existence of the psi phenomena, but because of the small sample size, the results were assessed as no better than by chance. Yet, there have been sufficient incidents, often from specific individuals who seem to have the exceptional power to see beyond their five senses, thus these experiments have continued. Now, Dean Radin (2006), the laboratory director of the Institute of Noetic Sciences, has performed a very large meta-analysis of these phenomena. He has examined a very large number of psi phenomena studies of seven different research designs for his statistical meta- analysis, e.g. whether information at a distance can be perceived in dreams, whether images can be received when sent by someone at a distance, detecting being stared at, influencing the roll of dice, and influencing the flip of a coin.

By collecting the available research data in each of these seven research designs and performing a meta-analysis of this research, the sample sizes become much larger, and because of this increase in sample size, even though the measured experimental effect in each design may be quite small, the effect becomes statistically significant. But even with a small effect in the direction of validating these psi phenomena, this analysis supports the reality of mental telepathy, clairvoyance, and psychokinesis. Assuming that our hunting and gathering ancestors were much better in going beyond the five senses than we are today because of the limitation of the rationality we have placed upon ourselves, this research provides us with hope that we can regain these powers.

Dream Psi

Psi experiences are those experiences that predict some future event, very often the death of someone important to the individual. One survey showed that about half of such psi experiences occur through nighttime dreams. In a typical dream psi experiment, a picture is repeatedly displayed throughout the night on a television monitor in a locked room with no one present. This picture was selected at random by a computer from a selection of pictures. The participant is asked to keep track of his or her dreams from throughout the night. The next morning, the participants upon going to the laboratory are shown four pictures, one being the target picture and are asked to rank the pictures with regard to how well they best represent their dreams. Radin found 47 such experimental studies that represented a total of 1270 trials. The odds against chance that the correct target picture was selected was 2.2×10^{10} to 1, thus the correct picture was selected better than by chance at over 22 billion to 1. When the participant is to select from four pictures, the target picture would be selected 25% of the time just by chance. The percentage of time that the correct picture is chosen would likely be above 25% yet quite close to 25%, and for a small sample size this would likely not be significant, but with 1270 trials, a relatively small increase in the percentage of correct selections becomes highly significant.

This experiment is traditionally repeated as a competitive exercise at the annual conference of the International Association for the Study of Dreams. The celebrated winner of the contest is the one whose dream best matches the target picture. I have found in my ecstatic trance workshops offered to the attendees of this conference that they are exceptionally receptive to the power of ecstatic trance as evident in their ability to experience the intent of each posture. By their attendance at the conference, they have shown that they value the altered state of consciousness of dreaming.

The Ganzfield Experiment

In the Ganzfield experiment, the *receivers* of an image sit relaxed in a soundproof room, with halved ping-pong balls over their eyes and wearing headphones that play a whooshing sound like the sound of a waterfall. A red light is shined that is seen through the ping-pong balls as a diffuse red glow. The sound and the red glow are in effect trance inducing. The *senders*, in a distant room, watch a repeated picture or a short video clip on a television monitor and are instructed to try to mentally send the picture or video to the *receiver*. This experimental setup typically last for a half hour, during which the *receiver* is to speak aloud what comes to his or her mind, words that are recorded. Then the *receiver* watches four videos or examines four pictures, one of which was the real target, and they are asked to rank the four based upon their impression of what they experienced. Again, selecting the correct picture by pure chance is 25%, or one time in four. For the meta-analysis of 88 studies that followed this design with a total of 3415 sessions, nearly 2.5 times more trials than for the dream psi experiments, the odds of selecting the correct picture or video was 3.0×10^{19} to 1. With the larger number of sessions, the odds of a correct response were greatly increased.

Psychokinesis

Radin performed meta-analyses on two psychokinetic designs, designs with distant intention, i.e. the intention to influence the outcome in the action of some non-living object such as the throw of a dice or the generation of random numbers.

Considering the outcome of the throw of a dice, with each throw the thrower focuses on one of the six sides of a dice, wishing for that side to come up, and the outcome is recorded as either a hit or a miss, i.e. whether the wished for side came up or didn't come up. For this design Radin found 169 reported studies with a total of 2.6 million dice tosses. With his meta-analysis he determined that the odds against chance in getting a hit was 2.6×10^{76} to 1.

In a similar design, but in wishing or calling for either a one or a zero from the random generation of ones and zeros, for the 595 studies that included 1.1 billion random events, the odds in getting a hit were 3052 to 1. These two studies validate the existence of the power of wishing for a particular outcome, even when the outcome is from some non-living object.

Unconscious Psychic Responses

So far with each design the results were examined from a conscious perspective, i.e. the receiver's awareness or lack of awareness of some distant stimulus. Radin examined two more designs that considered a physiological or unconscious reaction to some event, the effect of the event on the sweat glands, i.e. the galvanic skin response or GSR, an autonomic response to some message being sent from a distance, and to the event of being stared at.

In the first, the autonomic response to some message being sent from a distance, the receiver is placed in a solid steel, double-walled chamber that shields against electromagnetic signals and acoustic noise to ensure that no ordinary forces or signals can reach the receiver. The experimenter attaches wires to the receiver's fingers to monitor the changes in the activity of their sweat glands. Otherwise the receiver does nothing but sit in the comfortable reclining chair in the chamber.

The sender is taken to a distant, soundproofed room and sits in front of a video monitor and is instructed to follow what pops up on the monitor screen, either to mentally send a message to calm or to activate the receiver such as relaxing and taking a nap on a beach, or imagining running up a steep hill. The instruction lasts for about 20 seconds, and the sender is then to withdraw attention from the receiver and wait for the next trial. Over the course of 30 minutes the calming or activating instructions are presented randomly to the sender, for a total of 20 calming and 20 activating instructions.

For the meta-analysis of this design 40 studies were found with a total of 1055 trials. The odds against chance for the receiver to show a calming GSR response to the calming message and an activating response to the activating message were 1000 to one. Thus the message sent had a positive effective on the electrical conductivity of the receiver's skin moisture from the sweat glands, an autonomic response.

In a similar experiment but with remote staring only 15 studies were found with a total of 379 trials. Again the receiver sat comfortably in the chamber shielded against electromagnetic signals and acoustic noise while the sender in a distant room watched a monitor that randomly showed a closed-circuit television image of the receiver. The sender was instructed to stare intently at the image of the receiver when it appeared, otherwise when the screen went blank to relax and think about something else. With the 379 trials for this design the receiver showed a response through a change in the conductivity of skin moisture with the odds of 100 to 1, again demonstrating the presence of an autonomic response to being stared at from a distance.

Two Additional Studies

In considering unconscious responses beyond the autonomic response, Radin reported on two additional experimental designs that were not part of his meta-analysis, the effect on the central nervous system as seen in the receiver's electroencephalography, EEG, and the other on gut motility using electrogastrography, EGG.

In the first design that used EEG, the subjects of the experiment were pairs of people, twins, siblings, marriage partners, or parent–child. The members of a pair were at a geographic distance from each other. One of the pair's brain was stimulated with, for example, a flashing light, causing the brain to jump electrically in a predictable way. At the same time, the EEG of the distant partner in the pair was watched to see if it too jumped. Of the ten studies reported with this design eight were reportedly positive. This design has been repeated with similar pairs of people but with the sender believing that the partner in the pair was an unknown stranger. Again a response in the EEG of the partner was seen with the odds against chance of 50 to 1.

With regard to the experiment measuring gut motility or EGG, another unconscious response, the experiment was conducted in Radin's own laboratory. Again the design was similar to the one described above. The sender sat in front of two video monitors. The receiver's live video image was shown to the sender on one monitor and on the other was shown a sequence of emotional or neutral pictures. At the same time through a headset the sender listened to music matching the emotion or neutral nature of the picture. The emotional pictures and music were either positive such as smiling babies, kittens, or appetizing food, or negative evoking either anger or sadness such as a bomb exploding, pictures of a graveyard, or of unhappy people. The sender was to gaze at the image of the receiver while trying to send the emotion of the pictures and music seen in the other monitor. In between the sender was to relax and think about something else.

Again the pairs all knew each other, some casual friends others long-term partners. The receiver's gut or EGG response was significantly larger when the sender was sending an emotional response, with odds against chance of 167 to 1 for the positive emotions and 1100 to 1 for the angry or sad emotions.

This set of studies is quite amazing and strongly supports the existence of a mind beyond the one that relies upon the five senses, a mind that is extrasensory such as the one proposed by Laszlo that perceives through the cytoskeletal structure of the brain, which opens us to communing with the spirits of the universal mind. In the words of the Mi'kmaq Indian, Evan Pritchard, these "miracles don't violate laws of nature, they are the laws of nature," that within the Native American culture, "That's the way it works," (2013, p. 57).

This power of extrasensory perception has come very much alive for the participants of our ecstatic trance group. Repeatedly two or more members of the group have experiences that are connected in content. One recent occasion was when I experienced while in ecstatic trance a large orange moon filling the sky at the horizon, while the person I was facing saw a large wheel of orange cheese. On one occasion in the ecstatic group with eight participants, we broke up in four pairs, with the members of a pair facing each other as we went into trance. Though there were differences in the pairs of experiences there were astounding similarities. Both I and the person with whom I was paired experienced spiraling energy in our experiences. For another pair, they both were comfortably swimming underwater, and the third pair saw beams of blue, cool energy flowing, though their experiences were otherwise different. For the fourth couple, a husband and wife, the husband was walking on the beach holding his wife's hand, and the wife experienced her hand becoming very tired. Rather than experienced with occasional curiosity, such similarities in the ecstatic experiences of members of our group have become expected.

Braden's Divine Matrix

Gregg Braden offers another name for this *holographic matrix of in-formation*. He calls it *the Divine Matrix*, the container of information from the birth of the stars and for all time, the container that holds the universe and is the bridge between all things. He concludes from the research on DNA and from quantum physics research, that the particles of which we are made are in instantaneous communication with one another, can exist in two places at once, live in the past as well as the future, and even change history through choices in the present. Since we are composed of these particles, these attributes also apply to us. The only difference between those isolated particles and us is that we're made of a lot of them held together by the power of consciousness itself. In other words, Robert Lanza, MD, in his book *Biocentrism* (2009) develops seven principles of a new way of looking at everything in the universe from both the physical and living sides. His third principle is that the behavior of subatomic particles – indeed all particles and objects – is inextricably linked to the presence of an observer. Without the presence of a conscious observer, they at best exist in an undetermined state of probability waves.

Validation of this new understanding of life and the universe comes primarily from five research studies that Braden describes in his book, *The Divine Matrix*, three with DNA and two from quantum physics.

DNA Phantom Effect

This first study by Poponin and Gariaev explored the effect of DNA on photons (Braden, 2007, pp. 42–46). When the air was evacuated from a tube, the remaining photons within the vacuum were found to be everywhere within the tube, distributed in a random manner. When a sample of DNA was placed in the tube with the photons, rather than remaining scattered, the photons arranged themselves differently in the presence of this living material, arranged through what appeared to be an invisible force. Then when the DNA was removed, the photons remained ordered. The DNA and photons were still connected in some way.

The Effect of Emotions on Isolated DNA

In the second study performed by the Army, swabs of tissue and DNA collected from within the mouth were isolated from the person in another room, and held in a special chamber where the electrical conductivity of the DNA could be measured. The donor, several hundred feet away, was presented with video images that triggered specific emotions such as wartime footage, erotic images, or comedy. When the donor showed the emotional peaks and dips, the cells and DNA showed the same response.

When the Army's research ended, one researcher continued the study with up to 350 miles between the donor and the collected tissue and DNA. Even with this separation the emotions of the donor had the same instantaneous effect on this tissue and DNA sample.

The Effect of Coherent Emotions on Isolated DNA

Five people were trained in coherent emotions, i.e. a self-management technique of first quieting the mind, then shifting awareness to the heart and focusing on positive emotions, thus increasing the intensity of the emotion. This study was performed by the Institute of Heart Math, a group who was exploring how feeling originated from the heart. They recognized that an energy field around the heart was donut shaped, 5 to 8 feet in diameter. This heart field was referred to as the Torus and not considered an aura or prana. Again samples of DNA were taken from these five people and taken to a distant location, where the shape of the energy field of the sample of DNA was observed to change when the donor of the sample expressed an intensified emotion.

The Double Slit Experiment of Quantum Physics

This famous 1909 experiment performed by the British physicist Geoffrey Ingram Taylor involved the projection of a subatomic particle through a small hole in a barrier. When the particle passed through a slit and struck a target surface beyond the slit, as expected, it appeared as a particle. But with two slits in the barrier the particle passed through both slits at the same time and hit the target as if it was not a particle but a wave of energy that was somehow forced to travel as if it were a wave. The form of the barrier had an effect on the state of the particle. The conclusion is that sometimes electrons behave as we would expect of a particle, while at other times they may act as waves, thus a new rule is needed.

Also,

> Because it's assumed that the electron cannot really "know" anything in the truest sense of the word, the only other source of the awareness is the person watching the experiment. The conclusion here is that somehow the knowledge that the electron has two possible paths to move through is in the mind of the observer, and that the onlooker's consciousness is what determines how the electron travels.
>
> (Braden, 2007, p. 73)

But an observer is not supposed to have an effect on the results of the experiment, yet, in this case it did. The observer created a condition that affected the results. This supports the above stated third principle of biocentrism of Robert Lanza (2009).

From this perspective, it can be said that we have the ability to purposefully create the conditions of consciousness, whether through thoughts, feelings, emotions, or beliefs, which lock one possibility of our choosing into the reality. But it is not enough to simply say we choose a new reality, e.g. that we can function as two slits rather than one. The new reality depends upon the feeling that the new reality is accomplished, and it must be without ego and judgment. We must become in our lives the things that we choose to experience as our world.

Non-Local Coherence

In 1997 at the University of Geneva, scientists split a single photon into two separate particles, creating "twins" with identical properties. The two particles were then fired away from each other along a fiber-optic pathway to positions 14 miles separating one from the other. At the end of the path one was forced to choose between two random routes and, instantaneously, the other made the same turn. What affected one automatically affected the other in the same way. This continued connection between the two particles physicists call *quantum entanglement*, once connected always connected.

> The ancient mystics reminded our hearts, and modern experiments have proven to our minds, that the single most powerful force in the universe lives within each of us. And that is the great secret of creation itself: the power to create in the world what we imagine in our beliefs.
>
> (Braden, 2007, p. 210)

Applying this realization to cognitive therapy, to replace the old dysfunctional ways of thinking that are automatic or unconscious with the new healthier ways of thinking, choosing such change requires that we feel the new reality without ego or judgment, i.e. we must become in our lives the things we choose to experience as our world. To experience the new healthier thoughts in our lives they must become part of our automatic unconscious world.

We can access this divine matrix, as did our ancient ancestors in their visits to the spirit world. The divine matrix or the world of the spirits contains all information from the beginning of time, information that is available to us and can give us direction in life as it did for our ancestors if we will only open our minds to this possibility.

References

Braden, G. (2007). *The Divine Matrix: Bridging Time, Space, Miracles, and Belief.* Carlsbad, CA: Hay House.

Castaneda, C. (1987). *The Power of Silence: Further Lessons of Don Juan.* New York, NY: Simon & Schuster.

Gebser, J. (1984). *The Ever-Present Origin.* Athens, OH: Ohio University Press.

Lanza, R. (2009). *Biocentrism: How Life and Consciousness are the Keys to Understanding the True Nature of the Universe.* Dallas, TX: Benbella Books.

Lash, J. L. (2006). *Not in His Image: Gnostic Vision, Sacred Ecology, and the Future of Belief.* White River Junction, VT: Chelsea Green Publishing.

Laszlo, E. (2007). *Science and the Akashic Field: An Integral Theory of Everything.* Rochester, VT: Inner Traditions.

Laszlo, E. (2009). *The Akashic Experience: Science and the Cosmc Memory Field.* Rochester, VT: Inner Traditions.

Pritchard, E. T. (2013). *Bird Medicine: The Sacred Power of Bird Shamanism.* Rochester, VT: Bear & Co.

Radin, D. (2006). *Entangled Minds: Extrasensory Experiences in a Quantum Reality.* New York, NY: Paraview Pocket Books.

Sheldrake, R. (1995). *The Presence of the Past: Morphic Resonance and the Habits of Nature.* Rochester, VT: Park Street Press.

Waggoner, R. (2009). *Lucid Dreaming: Gateway to the Inner Self.* Needham, MA: Moment Point Press.

Wolchover, N. (2017). The Universe is as Spooky as Einstein Thought. *The Atlantic,* February 10.

9 Evolution of Consciousness

Over the past couple of hundred years psychologists and psychotherapists have been studying the human being, trying to understand the human's emotions, behavior, ways of thinking, perceiving, learning, etc., assuming that this understand comes from within the human's physical body, from within the confines of human skin. Now we realize that to understand the human being we must look beyond the physical body and into the mind beyond this body, the universal mind.

As we open ourselves to the world of the universal mind, a whole new way of understanding that which is happening around us is opening to us. We are now discovering that this world of the universal mind is not really new, because our hunter-gathering ancestors knew it well and relied upon it to give them direction in life. We lost touch with this world with the era of rational consciousness, when we believed that what was real was perceived only through the five senses, the senses of sight, sound, taste, smell, and touch. During this era of rationality we denied the reality of our sixth sense, the sense of intuition. Only now are we returning to the experiences of this sixth sense and discovering the value of what it has to offer us as it did our ancient ancestors of the archaic and magical era of consciousness. The world of our ancestors of the magical era was magical because of their ability to perceive this sixth sense, the ability to perceive beyond the five senses to experience the world beyond themselves, the world of the universal mind, the world of the spirits.

Those of the hunter-gathering cultures of today have retained this ability to access the world of the spirits, and it is up to us to regain this ability and to open ourselves to these spirits. As described in the previous chapter the existence of this extrasensory world is being validated scientifically and is accessed through the trance states of consciousness, altered states that suppress our rational mind, thus allowing us to experience the universal mind. My previous writings have shown the breadth of this world of the spirits, the spirits of our ancestors, the spirits of the Earth, spirits that provide healing and spirit journeying, the spirits of the future and spirits of metamorphosis, of shape-shifting to become the animal spirit guides that can lead us to new understanding of ourselves, the people around us, and of all life upon the Earth. My first book on ecstatic trance, *The Power of Ecstatic Trance* (2013), examines the ritual and the breadth of ways to use ecstatic trance. In my second book, *Baldr's Magic* (2014), I use ecstatic trance to commune with my Nordic ancestors. The third book, *Beowulf's Ecstatic Trance Magic* (2016a), takes us into the world of the spirits of the land with the example that leads us to better understand the world of the great Danish king, Hrothgar and his savior, Beowulf. My fourth book, *Trance Journeys of the Hunter-Gatherers* (2016b), visits the spirits of the Earth to show us how to live in oneness with the Earth. For the last 10,000 years we have become estranged from the magic of the living Earth through our attempts to control her. Now we are seeing how these attempts to control are destroying life on Earth as we know it, which is leading us to our own demise. Ecstatic trance can show us how to live in oneness as it did for our ancient hunting and gathering ancestors. These ancestors led a life of harmony by relating to all other life as sacred, their relatives upon which they depended. They were part of its evolution, not above it. Through ecstatic trance we can commune with these ancestors, learn how to emulate how they lived, and regain the ability to live sustainably with the Earth.

Time-Free Transparency

The five eras of consciousness as portrayed by Jean Gebser in his book, *The Ever-Present Origin* (1985), are a road map of this journey into the new age, the era of *Time-Free Transparency*. The first of these five eras of consciousness was the archaic era that began from about 160,000 to 200,000 years ago and lasted until approximately 10,000 years ago. This era was of the hunter-gatherers who lived basically in a dream world, in an altered state of trance. It was a world of magic, a world of communing with the animals as if they were their brothers and sisters. As this archaic era began to wind down, humans began to evolve into the second era, the era of *magical consciousness*, a world where they began to realize that they could see into the past and at a distance. When a hunting party was away from the village, those in the village could see and know where they were, and know of their success or the dangers of the hunt. The collected stories of Vine Deloria, the Native American storyteller and historian, offers many magical stories of the more contemporary hunter-gathering medicine men of North America. In this last book that he wrote before he died, *The World We Used to Live in* (2006, pp. 68–69), Deloria tells one especially memorable story of the medicine man, White Shield:

> A remarkable demonstration of the sacred stones of White Shield was related by Siya'ka. Siya'ka said that on one occasion he had lost two horses and asked White Shield to locate them. Before being bound with sinew, White Shield asked, "What sign shall the stone bring to show whether your horses are by a creek or on the prairie?" Siya'ka

replied: "If they are by a creek, let the stone bring a little turtle and a piece of clamshell, and if they are on the prairie let the stone bring a meadow lark."

White Shield then sent the stone on its quest. While the stone was absent the people prepared a square of finely pulverized earth ... It was evening when the stone returned. The tepee was dark as the fire had been smothered, but there was dry grass ready to put on it when White Shield ordered light. At last the stone appeared on the place prepared for it, and beside it was a little turtle with a small piece of clamshell in one of its claws.

After the appearance of the stone and verification of its powers, White Shield, without any apparent oral communication with the stone, told Siya'ka: "Your horses are 15 miles west of the Porcupine Hills at a fork of the Porcupine Creek. If you do not want to go for them there is a traveler coming that way who will get them and bring them in for you." This proved true. A neighbor of Siya'ka's had been out looking for wild fruit and on his way home he saw the horses at the fork of the Porcupine Creek, recognized them as Siya'ka's, and brought them back.

This magic is still available to us through the use of dreaming, hypnosis, and ecstatic trance if only we would cultivate it through practice.

Gebser's third era of consciousness is the era of mythic consciousness, the beginning of recorded history, the era when humans attempted to explain the creation, life, and the ways of nature through mythic stories or imaginative explanations. The new mythical stories were a step away from the magical experiences of the earlier era when the focus of consciousness was on experiencing the Earth and all of Earth's life. The new era, as human consciousness offered imaginative explanations for the Earth and its life, moved from experience to imagination.

Imagination is one avenue into the world of the unconscious and the universal mind, but the next era of rational consciousness takes us even further from the power found in the archaic and magical eras of consciousness. Gebser describes this rational era as beginning during the first millennium BC. Rationality limits our consciousness to that which is perceived by the five senses, thus disconnecting us from the unconscious mind and the universal mind. Only now that we are moving into the era of consciousness that opens us to the world of time-free transparency do we regain the power of the magical era, do we regain our *Ever-Present Origin*.

Developmental Stages of Human Consciousness

Gebser sees our consciousness mutating to a stage where we can now begin to access the universal mind, but this evolution requires that we mature to a level of spirituality that opens us to the beauty of the great diversity of all life on Earth. Our survival depends upon our recognition that in this diversity we are all deeply interdependent.

David Korten (2006, pp. 52–56) well describes our needed growth towards this level of spirituality in becoming an elder in leading others in the process of maturation. For us to really appreciate the world outside of our body, Korten has provided an outline of the developmental stages of human consciousness. The earliest stage of consciousness that he calls magical consciousness is the consciousness of our earliest years when we fantasize the world around us that is new to us, finding protection in this world with the help of our magical warriors such as Superman or Wonder Woman.

As we grow beyond this stage we grow into the world of our imperial consciousness when we seek power over our world by playing up to the powerful and exploiting the oppressed. Those who get stuck in this stage as they move into adulthood become greedy adults who seek accumulation of wealth that they consider a sign of the success in life. They are self-centered and self-absorbed. If they should seek therapy they may find resolution for their immediate emotional pain and emptiness, and can grow beyond their self-centeredness.

If they succeed in growing beyond their self-centeredness and begin to relate to and become empathetic to the feelings of others in their life, family, neighbors, associates, with greater rapport they begin to be seen as good citizens. This stage Korten calls socialized consciousness. They live in a small world of like-minded people who reinforce their way of thinking as they play by the rules of their identity group and expect fair reward. They are the majority of adults.

Those who develop beyond the stage of socialized consciousness become cultural creatives who are capable of living in a world inclusive of others who might think differently from them. They identify with life-affirming societies that work for the good of all. The cultural creative, a phrase coined by Paul Ray (2000), values embracing curiosity and concern for the world, its ecosystem and the diversity of its people, displaying an awareness of and activism on behalf of peace and social justice. Paul Ray estimates that these people are about a quarter of the adult population.

Finally the most mature, the fifth stage, are those with spiritual consciousness, the spiritual creatives who live in a complex and evolving world in which they engage as evolutionary co-creators. They become the elders and teachers in the new integral world that recognizes the interdependence of all creatures and substances of the Earth.

As a psychotherapist I recognized that the expectations of our current mental health system and of the insurance companies that may pay for therapy are satisfied with the resolution to the problems that have kept people in the second self-centered stage of consciousness, i.e. imperial consciousness, resolution that leads them to become socialized. The resolution of their problems opens these people to become good citizens in their small world of like-minded people. But for the future generation, for those who find themselves living in the new age of time-free transparency, more will be expected of them. Growth to become cultural and spiritual creatives with an elevated spiritual consciousness will be needed for the new age to flourish.

This growth to become spiritual creatives was evident in the vision of the ancient Gnostic mystery school of Egypt. As with the earlier hunter-gatherers, the Gnostics were adept in accessing the world of time-free transparency, the universal mind, the world of the spirits. They "were indeed experts in the cognitive and noetic sciences and adepts at parapsychology ... (cultivating) such detection to a fine art" (Lash, 2006, p. 191).

According to Abraham Maslow (1968), rather than to base psychological theory on cases of mental illness, it needs to be based on "peak experience," the best that humans have achieved, the ultimate. Maslow considers

> Humanistic, Third Force Psychology to be transitional, a preparation for a still "higher" Fourth Psychology that is transpersonal, transhuman, centered in the cosmos rather than in human needs and interests, and that goes beyond humanness, identity, self-actualization, and the like.
> (1968, pp. iii–iv)

In order to survive, we need to go beyond our current state of materialism that places us as humans at the end point of evolution to become transpersonal and transhuman by returning to our rightful place in the continuing process of evolution. "Materialistic people can be defined as those who do not recognize the true nature of the material world. This explains how a culture of rampant materialism can mindlessly destroy the natural resources of the planet we inhabit" (Lash, 2006, p. 206). Humanity needs "to participate wisely and lovingly in the web of life encompassing all species, and even to align itself with the planetary spirit, Gaia" (Lash, 2006, p. 156).

The New Age

Jean Gebser (1985) sees us moving into the era of time-free transparency, the fifth era of consciousness, the new age, but as with each of the previous transitions of moving into a new era, great turmoil and fighting will occur and is now again expected and occurring because of the threat felt by those hanging on for dear life to the old ways. In the 1949 words of Gebser,

> Soon we will witness the rise of some potentate or dictator who will pass himself off as the "savior" or healer and allow himself to be worshipped as such. But anyone who does this in the days to come, and is thereby confined to time and is visible in it, has nothing to do with the true manifestation of the one who, in time-free transparency, will make the future present.

This turmoil is quite evident at this time in history and portends the coming of this new age. Laszlo and Dennis (2013) believe that this transition will be evident and at a point of no return by the year 2020.

What is this new age, and what can we expect of it? According to Gebser, it is the age of time-free transparency when we can again commune with the spirits. David Korten (2006) describes it as the age of the spiritual creative. But there are numerous other descriptions of it. I have attempted to list a few of the changes expected in the new age, but I know this list of five elements is quite incomplete.

- Oneness with the Earth: We will no longer see ourselves as superior to all other life and that which is of the Earth. We will treat all that is of the Earth with respect. We will recognize that the Earth is alive and everything of the Earth is interdependent, i.e. Gaia, that the Earth does and will sustain us, and we will again realize that we need to give back to her as much, if not more, than we take. We are still learning how to do this, but one beginning step is seen in our striving to garden organically. Another important step is to rediscover that which our hunting and gathering ancestors knew well and that is to listen to the spirits of our ancestors and the Earth that are alive and exist all around us. Thomas Berry's writings well portray the importance of this sense of oneness with the Earth (1988), and Richard Tarnas (2006) has the hope that we will rediscover the world soul or the *anima mundi* and will no longer feel separated from the enchantment of the Earth. The ecology movement has begun in carrying us in this direction with a great diversity in the actions we may take, recycling, avoiding excessive packaging and consumption, living organically, decreasing our carbon footprint, expanding the use of renewable energy, but there is much more. Especially important is changing our attitude by leaving behind our belief in our superiority, and rejoining the rest of the creatures of the Earth.
- Sense of Community: We all need to work together, share without greed, and care for each other in mutual support. This includes all life below, upon, and above the Earth. Again we are all one and interdependent, and when one suffers we all suffer. The village life of our hunting and gathering ancestors of working and sharing together provides us with an exceptionally clear vision as to how we can live together in community. Felicitas Goodman (1988), in summarizing the research on Stone Age economics of Marshall Sahlins (1972), writes:

> In a very real way, the hunters and gatherers open the first chapter of our human history. And fittingly, this dawning was as close to paradise as humans have ever been able to achieve. The men did the hunting

and scavenging, working for about three hours a week, and the women took care of daily sustenance by gathering vegetal food and small animals. It was such a harmonious existence, such a successful adaptation, that it did not materially alter for many thousands of years. This view is not romanticizing matters. Those hunter-gatherer societies that have survived into the present still pursue the same lifestyle, and we are quite familiar with it from contemporary anthropological observation. Despite the unavoidable privations of human existence, despite occasional hunger, illness, and other trials, what makes their life-ways so enviable is the fact that knowing every nook and cranny of their home territory and all that grows and lives in it, the bands make their regular rounds and take only what they need. By modern calculations this amounts to only about 10% of the yield, easily recoverable under undisturbed conditions, because they do not aspire to controlling their habitat, they are a part of it.

- A Sense of Harmony and Peace: Our mutual respect for each other in our great diversity brings us a sense of harmony and peace. Each of us has that which is valuable to the whole, to Gaia, to share, and our mutual caring for each other brings us peace and harmony. We are all one and all have something important to offer. Barbara Hand Clow (2007) in her writings has shown us of this potential for harmony and peace as we move into the era of the Homo Pacem. Carl Johan Calleman (2004) describes the world that we now live in as one of dualistic thinking, automatic ways of thinking that have been our survival in this world of separation, separation so deep within us that it blocks our true connection to the Earth and the community of all life on Earth. Unlearning that which separates us will bring us into the new world of harmony and peace. Charles Eisenstein (2013) describes in great detail the world of separation that keeps us tied to our dualistic thinking and what is needed for us to break free of it.
- A Sense of Curiosity and Learning: We are on a journey into this new age and we are far from having all the answers as how to live in oneness, harmony, and peace, and with a sense of community. Our minds need to remain open in curiosity and in learning, learning from each other in our great diversity as how to live. We need to listen openly to our ancestral spirits and the spirits of the Earth that are available to us from beyond our five senses, from our dreams and other altered states of consciousness such as hypnotic and ecstatic trance. Sergio Magaña (2012, p. 44), a Toltec teacher in the shamanic lineage of dreaming knowledge, proclaims that "If we fail to understanding the meaning of the original language, any attempt to appreciate the great change that we are going to live through will be a useless exercise."

- A Sense of Creativity: In living in harmony and peace with a sense of curiosity and openness to learn from the diversity of all life, we go beyond the destructiveness we have imposed on the Earth and each other. We are discovering a new sense of creative beauty, of new ways of caring for ourselves, for all life, and the Earth in ways that bring about a growing sense of beauty of all that is around us. Drawing from the matriarchal lifeway of our ancient hunting and gathering ancestors, Riane Eisler (1988) shows us how the veneration of the Mother Goddess who brings us life, our great mother Earth can bring us into a world of creativity rather than destruction. This sense of creativity goes hand in hand with time-free transparency or the use of ecstatic trance. From my experience with ecstatic trance I find that the artist and those who value their dreams are way ahead of others in the fullness in which they embrace ecstatic trance. They find in ecstatic trance broad new visions in their creativity and artistic expression.

The ancient hunter-gatherers lived a life of much greater uniformity, a life where everyone within a particular age and gender group offered the same thing to their community. There was not the great diversity that there is today, especially now with the ease of communication that exists between the various ethnic groups around the world. This diversity brings about much of the alienation and tension we are experiencing, and the current political administration feeds on this alienation by placing being white and male above everything else. But the diversity within our country and the world can and needs to be valued and appreciated. The breadth of knowledge is now so great that one person can no longer know everything, thus we are dependent upon others with this diversity of knowledge to show us what we need to know and how to live. The valuing and veneration of this diversity is especially important when we realize that we do not have dominion over the Earth, but that we are no better than or lesser than all other life, that all life has much to teach us as we live in oneness with it. Our delusional belief that we have dominion over the Earth has brought us to a point of near extinction. We are beginning to discover the way to live by observing other life on Earth, e.g. when we recognize that planting our gardens with a diversity of plants creates a healthier and more prosperous garden than does a monoculture.

To succeed in attaining this new age we need to move beyond the life stage of socialized consciousness and into the world of the cultural and spiritual creative. Expanding cognitive-behavioral therapy beyond its limited objectivist approach for changing our dysfunctional way of thinking to incorporate the constructivist approach that provides the needed understanding of *why* we were stuck in our dysfunctional way of thinking, behaving, and feeling, can carry us into the world of the cultural and spiritual creative.

References

Berry, T. (1988). *The Dream of the Earth*. San Francisco, CA: Sierra Club Books.

Brink, N. E. (2013). *The Power of Ecstatic Trance: Practices for Healing, Spiritual Growth, and Accessing the Universal Mind*. Rochester, VT: Bear & Co.

Brink, N. E. (2014). *Baldr's Magic: The Power of Norse Shamanism and Ecstatic Trance*. Rochester, VT: Bear & Co.

Brink, N. E. (2016a). *Beowulf's Ecstatic Trance Magic: Accessing the Archaic Powers of the Universal Mind*. Rochester, VT: Bear & Co.

Brink, N. E. (2016b). *Trance Journeys of the Hunter-Gatherers: Ecstatic Practices to Reconnect with the Great Mother and Heal the Earth*. Rochester, VT: Bear & Co.

Calleman, C. J. (2004). *The Mayan Calendar and the Transformation of Consciousness*. Rochester, VT: Bear & Co.

Clow, B. H. (2007). *The Mayan Code: Time Acceleration and Awakening the World Mind*. Rochester, VT: Bear & Co.

Deloria, V. (2006). *The World We Used to Live in: Remembering the Powers of the Medicine Men*. Golden, CO: Fulcrum Publishing.

Eisenstein, C. (2013). *The Most Beautiful World Our Hearts Know Is Possible*. Berkeley, CA: North Atlantic Books.

Eisler, R. (1988). *The Chalice and the Blade: Our History, Our Future*. San Francisco, CA: Harper One.

Gebser, J. (1985). *The Ever-Present Origin*. Athens, OH: Ohio University Press.

Goodman, F. (1988). *Ecstasy, Ritual, and Alternate Reality: Religion in a Pluralistic World*. Bloomington, IN: Indiana University Press.

Korten, D. (2006). *The Great Turning: From Empire to Earth Community*. San Francisco, CA: Berrett-Koehler Publishing.

Lash, J. L. (2006). *Not in His Image: Gnostic Vision, Sacred Ecology, and the Future of Belief*. White River Junction, VT: Chelsea Green Publishing.

Laszlo, E., and Dennis, K. (2013). *Dawn of the Akashic Age: New Consciousness, Quantum Resonance, and the Future of the World*. Rochester, VT. Inner Traditions.

Magaña, S. (2012). *2012–2021: The Dawn of the Sixth Sun*. Torino, Italy: Blossoming Books.

Maslow, A. (1968). *Toward a Psychology of Being*. New York, NY: Van Nostrand Reinhold Company.

Ray, P. H. (2000). *The Cultural Creatives: How 50 Million People Are Changing the World*. New York, NY: Three Rivers Press.

Sahlins, M. (1972). *Stone Age Economics*. New York, NY: Aldine Publishing Co.

Tarnas, R. (2006). *Cosmos and Psyche: Intimations of a New World View*. New York, NY: Penguin Books.

Index

Aaroz, D. 7, 47
absence of mutual contradictions *see* metaphoric language
affect bridge 5–6, 56–59, 62, 66, 97, 99–100
age regression 5, 56, 58–59, 97
Akashic field 27, 104, 107
Alladin, A. 49
Amy 2, 4–9, 21–22, 26, 36–38
analytic hypnotherapy 6–7, 47–48, 51, 54, 56–68, 83, 84, 94–98, 103
anger management 50–51
anxiety 2–3, 6, 8, 22, 37, 43, 46–48, 52–53, 57, 65, 99–100
Apostolic Church 69–70
archaic era 120–124
asymmetrical logic *see* metaphoric language
automatic thought 2–11, 26, 30–31, 49

Bahia Posture 79–80, *80*
Barber, T. 41
Barnett, E. 56
Baudouin, C. 7
Bear Spirit Posture 84–85, *85*, 90, 97, 99, 102
Beck, A. 1–4, 8, 12n, 25–26, 31–32, 45, 50
Bernheim, H. 42
Berry, T. 124
biocentrism 115–117
bodily felt sense *see* Gendlin, E.
body postures 71–72
Bowers, K. 46–47
Braden, G. 104, 115–117

Bulkeley, K. 18
Burns, D. 49

Calleman, C. J. 125
calling the spirits 70–71, 90, 96, 102
Campbell, Jean 15
Campbll, Joseph 3, 79
Castaneda, C. 95, 109
catharsis 6, 56–57
celebration postures *see* body postures
Chapman, R. A. 47–51
Chuck 98–102
clairvoyance *see* Radin, D.
Clow, B. H. 125
cognitive behavioural hypnotherapy 51–54
cognitive-narrative dreamwork 22–23
collective unconscious 12, 15, 79
concentrated attention 31–33
condensation *see* metaphoric language
confusion 31, 41
corrective emotional experience 1, 6–8, 28, 54, 56–57, 61
cultural creative *see* developmental stages of consciousness
cultural diversity 98
Cuyamungue Institute 84
cytoskeletal structure 108, 114

death-rebirth postures *see* body postures
Deloria, V. 120
depression 3, 8, 17, 21–22, 30–35, 48–50, 57, 65–68, 72
developmental stages of consciousness 121–123

disorientation 31, 41
displacement *see* metaphoric language
divination postures *see* body postures
divine matrix 115–117
Dowd, T. 50–51
Doweiko, H. 26
dream incubation 18–20
dream psi *see* Radin, D.
dysfunctional thinking 4, 9, 17, 54

ecstatic soul retrieval 51, 69, 84–103
ecstatic trance 5, 10–11, 16, 19, 35–36, 48, 69–83, 84–103, 107, 109, 111, 114, 120–121, 125–126
Eisenstein, C. 125
Eisler, R. 126
Emerson, V. F. 71
empathetic resonance 107
evolution 105–106; co-creator 12; of consciousness 119–126
exposure and response prevention *see* cognitive-behavioural hypnotherapy

Feathered Serpent Posture 87, 90, 94, 98, 102
Feinstein, D. 14, 34
felt shift *see* Gendlin, E.
first order change *see* Rosner, R. & Lyddon, W.
focused attention 3, 5, 31, 32
Freud, S. 11, 14

Ganzfield experiment *see* Radin, D.
Gebser, J. 69, 79, 106, 120–124
Gendlin, E. 24, 32
Ginandes, C. 47
Goodman, F. 69–72
guided imagery 5, 10, 38–39, 48, 64–65, 103

Hallstatt Warrior Posture 76, 77, 78
Hameroff, S. & Penrose, R. 108
Hammond, C. 47
healing postures *see* body postures
holographic matrix 27, 104, 108, 115
hypnosis 3, 5, 7, 9–11, 33, 41–54, 56–68, 81, 95, 104, 121
hypnotic desensitization 47

hypnotic mind-set 41–42

ideomotor signaling 59
imagery rehearsal therapy 21, 34
imagination 9–11, 21–22, 34–35, 45–47, 67, 121; law of reverse effect 7
imperial consciousness *see* developmental stages of consciousness
initiation posture *see* body postures
intent 18, 76, 95, 111

Jama Coaque Diviner Posture 81, 82
Javel, A. F. 11, 14
Jivaro Underworld Posture 87, 89, 93, 97–98, 101

kindling 3, 6, 49, 105
Kirsch, I. 46
Kitaev, A. and Pitkanen, M. 107
Korten, D. 12, 68, 76, 121–124
Krakow, B. 21–22, 24, 34
Krippner, S. 14, 34

Lady of Cholula Posture 86, 86, 87, 93, 97, 99, 101
Lanza, R. 115, 117
Larsen, S. & Verner, T. 15, 19–20
Lash, J. L. 109, 123
Laszlo, E. 27, 75, 104, 107–110, 114
Laszlo, E. & Dennis, K. 124
latent dreams 14
law of reverse effect 7, 47
left-hemispheric functioning 47
lower world postures *see* body postures

Magaña, S. 125
magical consciousness *see* developmental stages of consciousness
magical era 119–124
Mair, L. P. 73
manifest dreams 14
Matt 30–31, 33–35, 66–68
mental telepathy *see* Radin, D.
metaphoric language 9–11, 16–17, 26
metamorphosis postures *see* body postures
middle world postures *see* body postures
Molly 23–27, 30, 32, 38–40, 44–45, 57–65

morning reverie 18–19, 35–36, 64, 66
morphic field 104–107
morphic resonance 105–106
mythic era 119–121, 123–124

non-local coherence 104, 106, 110, 117
Nupe Diviner Posture 73, 73

obesity 46
obsessive compulsive disorders 9
Olmec Diviner Posture 87, 88, 88
Olmec Prince Posture 87, 91, 93

parasympathetic nervous system 95
Patricia 89–96
Pete 45
phobias 8–9, 47–48
Piaget, J. 4
Poponin, P. and Garajaev, V. 115
Pritchard, E. 114
problem solving therapy *see* cognitive-behavioural hypnotherapy
psychokinesis *see* Radin, D.

quantum entanglement 104, 117
quantum physics 104, 106, 110, 115–116

Radin, D. 104, 110–114
rational era 69, 75, 79, 107, 111, 119, 120–121, 123–124
Ray, P. H. 65, 122
Rayner, E. 10
realm of the inorganic beings 95
relaxation 43, 46–49, 52, 95–97; depth 42; soul retrieval 99, 102
remembering dreams 18
replacement of external by internal reality *see* metaphoric language
Robertson, J. 3, 9, 42, 51–53
Rogers, C. 42
Rosner, R. 15, 21–26, 32, 34
Rosner, R. & Lyddon, W. 25

Sahlins, M. 124
Salmen, K. 84
Schempp, W. 107
second order change *see* Rosner, R & Lyddon, W.

self-hypnosis 35, 36–38
shape-shifting postures *see* body postures
Sheldrake, R. 75, 104–107
Siya'ka 120–121
smoking addition 73–74
smudging 70, 75, 96
socialized consciousness *see* developmental stages of consciousness
speaking in tongues 69–70
spirit guides 75, 85, 87, 93, 96, 102, 119
spirits world 28, 35–36, 75, 95, 104, 106–107, 114, 117, 119–124; ancestral 69, 76–77, 125; earth spirits 69, 79–83, 125
spiritual creative *see* developmental stages of consciousness
stalking 95
stress inoculation training *see* cognitive-behavioural hypnotherapy
suggestibility 42
symmetrical logic *see* metaphoric language
sympathetic nervous system 95

time-free-transparency 106, 120–124
timelessness *see* metaphoric language

unconscious psychic response *see* Radin, D.
underworld postures *see* body postures
upper world postures *see* body postures

Venus of Galgenberg Posture 88, 92

Waggoner, R. 27, 108–109
Watkins, J. 6, 56, 58
what? 4, 5, 11, 54, 56, 60
White Shield 120–121
why? 4–6, 8–9, 11, 26, 44, 47–56, 59, 62, 74, 83, 127
will power 7, 47
Wolchover, N. 104
Wolpe, J. 47
working through 11

Yapko, M. 50
yes-set 9, 11, 26, 30, 40–45, 47–58, 61–62, 96, 100